HORSE RACING

The Last 25 Years

HORSE RACING

The Last 25 Years

HOWARD WRIGHT

WHSMITH
EXCLUSIVE
· BOOKS ·

This edition published by W H Smith Ltd 1992

Produced by
Book Connections Limited
47 Norfolk Street, Cambridge CB1 2LE

ISBN 0 906782 94 5

A CIP catalogue record for this book is available from the British Library.

Designer – Jim Reader
Editorial Manager – Roz Williams
Photo Researcher – Sarah Wombwell
Production Manager – Debbie Wright

Typeset in Palatino and Frutiger
Origination by Koford International, Singapore
Printed by Proost N.V., Turnhout, Belgium

Acknowledgements

The author and publishers wish to thank the following for the use of photographs:

P Bertrand et fils 15, 31, 108-9, 115

Gerry Cranham 9, 17, 22-3, 24 (top), 25, 26, 27, 29, 32-3, 34, 38, 39, 52-3, 57, 62 (left), 63, 75, 76, 77 (both), 79, 81, 83 (bottom), 85 (left), 88, 91 (bottom), 93, 121, 123, 134, 143, 144, 145

Express Newspapers 106-7

Alan Johnson 45, 50, 68, 73 (left), 86-7, 102-3, 142, 154

Trevor Jones Front cover, 10-11, 24 (bottom), 40-1, 44, 48, 49, 51, 52, 59, 61, 62 (right), 70, 73 (right), 83 (top), 84, 85 (right), 89, 90, 91 (top), 92, 94 (both), 95, 96, 97 (bottom), 98, 147, 151, 152, 153, 155, 157 (both)

Lensmen 128-9

News International 136

Press Association 54, 55, 114, 118

Racing Post 64-5

Alec Russell Back cover, 69, 78, 112, 120, 130, 135, 140, 150

George Selwyn 36, 37, 41, 42, 46-7, 56, 58, 60, 72, 74, 82, 97 (top), 99, 100, 101 (both), 125, 126-7, 133, 138, 146-7, 148, 149, 156

Sport & General Press Agency Ltd 12, 13, 14, 16, 18, 19, 20 (both), 21, 30, 35, 43, 66, 67 (both), 71, 80, 104, 105, 107, 110-11, 111, 113, 116, 117, 119, 124, 137, 139, 141

Sporting Pictures (UK) Ltd 131

They would also like to thank Jenny Knight for her careful editing, proofreading and indexing, and John Randall for authenticating the text.

Contents

INTRODUCTION

A trip to Chester for the three-day meeting in May is the best way of savouring the whole history of horseracing in Britain. There has been racing here since 1540 but, like the sport as a whole, Chester has been witness to more changes in the last 25 years than in any other similar period. It has not all been change for the better, but it has been all change nevertheless.

The biggest single development has been the spread of international influence; the world of racing has become a much smaller place in the last 25 years. Take a race at Chester in 1991, for instance.

Toulon won what used to be called the Chester Vase. Now it's the Dalham Chester Vase, sponsored by members of the Maktoum family from Dubai who own the Dalham Hall Stud in Newmarket. Toulon was trained in France by Andre Fabre and ridden by Pat Eddery, an Irishman based in Britain. The horse is owned by Khalid Abdullah, an Arab businessman whose racing interests are spread far and wide. And Toulon was the product of a sire (Top Ville) who had a mix of British and French parentage, and a dam (Green Rock) who was born in France but was conceived in England from American parents, one of whom (Mill Reef) proved among the outstanding horses of the age, winning the top races in England and France.

If that sounds complicated, it is. But within a single example can be found many of the strands which have gone to make up the major changes of the last 25 years.

Vastly improved communications have made it a simple matter for horses to be flown across the Channel, across the Atlantic and even across to the other side of the world. With the money to spend, top European buyers are as likely to be seen at yearling sales in Kentucky as they are at Newmarket or in Ireland and France. American-bred horses are commonplace. Overseas-based owners have become just as familiar, though the names may change over the years.

The new boys seek success at the top end, the best races, which have been sorted out into a recognized pecking order called the Pattern system. This involves an agreement between the major countries of Europe – Britain, Ireland, France, Germany and Italy – which have worked out a programme of top races through the season, arranged into three groups. The Dalham Chester Vase is in Group 3; the Ever Ready Derby is in Group 1.

The Pattern system has become a credible means of bringing together the best horses; it acts like a series of European Cup football matches, except that the 'teams' decide whom they will play against. If they want to avoid each other, so be it; but if they want to win the biggest prizes, they have to face the big guns.

But Europe is not the only goal. The United States is just a few hours away by jet, and the Breeders' Cup meeting, run for the first time in 1984 and offering a total of $10 million in prize-money for its mix of turf and dirt races, has become an irresistible magnet. Other US race tracks have cottoned on to the opportunities, and they aim to catch the late-season horses whose owners may be tempted to leave them on foreign soil, where the rewards can be out of this world.

Around the other side of the globe, Japan and Hong Kong have also sent out invitations, tempting European owners to race for untold wealth in yen and dollars. Though the level of Japanese interest seems to fluctuate, they have long been buyers of stallions from Europe – it is usually one-way traffic.

The effect of these home thoughts for abroad is that the seasons have been turned around for some of the best horses. Previously they started work early in the year in Europe, reached their first peak around Derby time, and returned for a big race in September or early October. Now there is a growing tendency for summer holidays to start in mid-July and last until the end of September, and autumn becomes a time to show their renewed mettle, first in Europe and then in the States, or beyond.

Group 1 races and trips to faraway places are, naturally, for the minority; that much has not changed. Despite its pitfalls, racehorse ownership remains a popular pastime and there are more horses in training in Britain than ever before. Equally, there are fewer people able to lay claim to a whole horse, and the number of syndicates and partnerships has increased. Company ownership grew rapidly in the boom years of the 1980s but has been one of the casualties of recession. Old-style, large-scale owner-breeders, once the backbone of British racing, have lost a lot of their muscle, forced to review the situation in the face of taxation and unable to compete in the high-powered world of stallion syndication. Several have sold their studs to the Arabs.

There is still a place for the small owner with a cheap horse, but he has found it increasingly difficult to break into the big time. Money might not guarantee success, but it helps. Only in the National Hunt field can the small man hope occasionally to hit the jackpot. Sirrell Griffiths struck a huge blow here when Norton's Coin, one of three horses he trained on his farm in Wales, ventured out early one morning to win the Cheltenham Gold Cup.

The passing of the major owner-breeders, and their succession by a handful of multi-horsepower owners, has affected training patterns. Despite the overwhelming odds against success, there seems no shortage of people willing to try their hand at training. The north finds it hard to compete, except in National Hunt; and concentration of ownership into a few, large training stables has thrust younger men, entrusted with Arab interests, to the forefront. They have taken their places alongside established trainers who joined the Middle East payroll from the late 1970s.

As an example, four Newmarket trainers – Cecil, Cumani, Gosden and Stoute – started 1992 with an average of 160 horses under their care, while relative newcomers Alex Scott and Alec Stewart had 90 and 70. Elsewhere, Messrs Dunlop and Cole averaged 130. In each case an Arab is signing most of the cheques for their training bills. Little wonder the racing world marvels at Richard Hannon, who trained 126 winners in 1991 and started the next season with a stable of 140 – and not one Arab owner.

The trend has moved into the riding academy, and the most successful Flat jockeys in Britain – Eddery, Carson, Cauthen, Swinburn, and even rising star Munro – are now retained by major owners, not trainers. In National Hunt, Peter Scudamore has brought a fresh interpretation to the word record, thanks to his link with Martin Pipe.

Over the years racecourses have come and gone but, perhaps surprisingly, only four have closed in the last 25 years, compared with nine between 1960 and 1965. Despite occasional threats from the racing authorities to withdraw support, and more regular criticism that there are too many racecourses in Britain, only Alexandra Park (1970), Wye (1974), Lanark (1977) and Stockton (1981) have shut up shop. Many more courses have undergone extensive renovation; all are having to look to greater usage on non-racing days for survival. The

Desert Orchid proves that whatever else changes in racing, horses will always be its great attraction.

arrival of all-weather track racing has given two courses – Lingfield Park and Southwell – something extra to think about, and the decision to stage two experimental Sunday meetings in 1992 will give them all a peep into the future.

Administration has moved on from the days when the Jockey Club was all-powerful. It remains a potent body of influence, but the Levy Board, which looks after money collected by the bookmakers from punters' bets, and the Horseracing Advisory Council, representing all the sectional interests, have developed important roles. Moves towards establishing a British Racing Authority to provide better control are in their early stages.

Betting too has advanced over the last 25 years, fuelled by the growth of major bookmaking chains, which have to watch the needs of their shareholders as closely as the requirements of their customers. Televised racing in betting shops, daily bringing live pictures from all parts of the country, has been the biggest development; evening opening may be the next.

The racecourses' staple diet, the racing itself, has undergone subtle changes, echoing in part the international trend already noted. Variety remains the major attraction in Britain but on the Flat there has been a gradual tendency to attach most importance to races over ten and 12 furlongs, while staying races have lost much of their glamour. Sponsorship has blossomed, so that most of the major races – outside that last bastion of propriety, Royal Ascot – have a company's name attached, and there is consternation and even panic among racecourse executives if the stock market threatens to dip a point or two. Traditionalists believe this is an unhealthy trend and look forward to the day when the Derby reverts officially to being the Derby; Epsom does not necessarily agree.

Sponsorship by private companies has been one of the key elements in the growth of National Hunt racing over the last 25 years – television coverage, increased media attention, even support by the Queen Mother, are others. Continuity has also played an important part. National Hunt horses stay around longer, providing they steer clear of injury, so the public has time to take an Arkle, Red Rum or Desert Orchid to their hearts. Flat horses are gone all too quickly these days.

But whichever code, Flat or jumping, takes the public's fancy, the horse remains the most important common denominator. Without the horse racecourses would be out of business; there would be nothing to own, nothing to train and nothing to ride, and whatever else the bookmakers found to bet on, it would be far less interesting. This review of the last 25 years is essentially a celebration of the racehorse.

AL
EVER READY
AL
EVER READY

Great Horses

Everyone who follows horseracing has one favourite horse, as well as a collection of other favourite horses. But who can accurately define a Great Horse?

Racing fans tend to look no further than the moment and we have seen more 'great' horses than we deserve. Down the years many horses have been deemed to be great, only to have their limitations exposed when conditions change. That need not be the horse's fault; more than likely we were wrong to overrate him.

In one respect racing has the advantage over most other sports in determining greatness. It has a number of rating systems which are designed to lay down an order of merit each year. One is official, being produced by Flat-race handicappers from the leading European countries, and known as the International Classifications; others are published by private companies and individuals.

These are the best guides to the great horses of the age, and a deal of notice has been taken of them in compiling this list of 20 Great Horses, who range across Britain, France, Ireland and the United States, and Flat and jumping.

But the rankings are still matters of opinion, even if they have the authority of individuals who spend their working lives poring over results, tables and charts of pounds and lengths. And that leaves room for other opinions. Some of them have been expressed in choosing the following Top Twenty.

If your favourite horse is not here, apologies. If it is, congratulations on your excellent judgement.

Sir Ivor

Born 1965. By Sir Gaylord out of Attica, by Mr Trouble.
Owned: Raymond Guest. Trained: Vincent O'Brien, in Ireland.

Lester Piggott uses Sir Ivor's brilliant speed to cut down Connaught in the Derby.

Sir Ivor could have been paid no higher compliment than to be described by Lester Piggott as his favourite horse among the record nine Derby winners he rode. Yet he was also the horse who brought Piggott a roasting from American journalists ... for winning!

Sir Ivor ended his 13-race career in November 1968 at Laurel in the Washington DC International, the world's first truly

international horserace. Having been boxed on the rails along the back stretch, Sir Ivor was presented with an opening a furlong from the winning post and he took it in an instant. Once in front, Sir Ivor settled the issue in a matter of strides, and Piggott eased him near the finish, winning by just under a length. It might not have been one of Piggott's best riding performances – he was perhaps fortunate to find an opening when he did – but it was a brilliant exhibition of speed from Sir Ivor. Yet the local journalists were not impressed, and at the post-race Press conference they rounded on Piggott for making a good horse look like a moderate one.

Nothing could have been further from the truth. Sir Ivor was not just a good horse; he was an outstanding one, with a burst of speed that separated him from all but Vaguely Noble among his generation. It was the hallmark of a career that had the word 'international' written all over it.

Bred in the United States and bought there for $42,000 on behalf of Raymond Guest, one-time US Ambassador to Ireland, he was trained in Ireland by the peerless Vincent O'Brien. Sir Ivor won two of Europe's best juvenile races – the National Stakes in Ireland and the Grand Criterium at Longchamp – and among five wins as a three-year-old he impressively beat Petingo in the 2,000 Guineas, ruthlessly cut down Connaught in the Derby, easily landed the odds in the Champion Stakes and, as related, returned to his native country as the first Derby winner to race in the States since Papyrus and his ill-starred excursion in 1923.

The fact that Sir Ivor lost four times between the Derby and the Champion Stakes was disappointing at the time, but it made not a jot of difference to his reputation at the end of the season, by which time he had comfortably erased any stigma of defeat.

Owner Guest had previously won the Derby with Larkspur, and was to complete a rare big-race double when L'Escargot won both the Grand National and the Cheltenham Gold Cup. He showed his appreciation for European racing by allowing Sir Ivor two seasons at stud in Ireland, where his produce included the Derby runner-up Cavo Doro (bred by Lester Piggott) and the champion southern hemisphere stallion Sir Tristram. Sir Ivor was repatriated in 1971 to stand at Claiborne Farm and by the time of his retirement in the summer of 1991 his most outstanding produce, mainly fillies, included the six-times Grade 1 winner Optimistic Gal and the champion older horse Bates Motel, as well as a host of successful broodmares.

Raymond Guest was one of racing's lucky owners. As well as Sir Ivor, the Grand National and Cheltenham Gold Cup winner L'Escargot carried his colours.

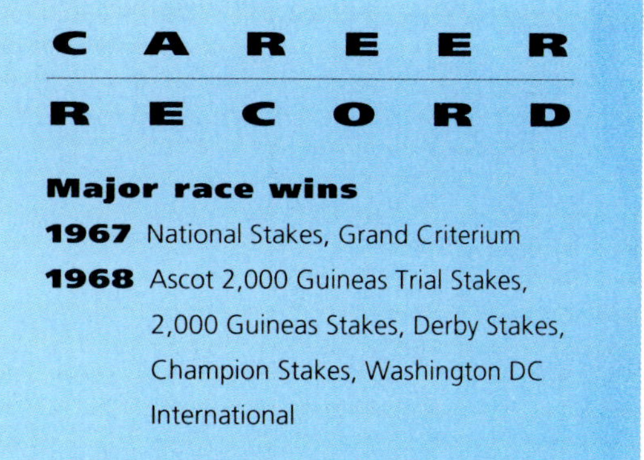

CAREER RECORD

Major race wins

1967 National Stakes, Grand Criterium

1968 Ascot 2,000 Guineas Trial Stakes, 2,000 Guineas Stakes, Derby Stakes, Champion Stakes, Washington DC International

VAGUELY NOBLE

Born 1965. By Vienna out of Noble Lassie, by Nearco.
Owned: L Brook Holliday; Robert and Wilma Franklyn, and Nelson Bunker Hunt. Trained: Walter Wharton; Etienne Pollet, in France.

Racing is built partly on the urge to gamble, and one of the biggest in recent years was taken in December 1967, when Robert and Wilma Franklyn paid 136,000 guineas at Tattersalls Sales in Newmarket for Vaguely Noble and shortly afterwards sold a half-share to the under-bidder Nelson Bunker Hunt.

The final bid was a world record for a thoroughbred at public auction, eclipsing the 67-year-old British record, which stood at 37,500 guineas. It was set for a colt rated only 1lb off the best, who had won his last two races in good class by 12 lengths and seven lengths, but who had one major drawback. Following the death of Vaguely Noble's owner-breeder Lionel Holliday before the colt was a year old, he had not been entered for the Classics. He would have to win the Prix de l'Arc de Triomphe as a three-year-old to be worth the money.

Vaguely Noble did win the Arc. More than that, he beat one of the best fields ever to take part in the Longchamp race, which has emerged over the last 25 years as Europe's most important middle-distance event.

He had shown as a two-year-old that resolute galloping was his strong suit, and it took him right to the top in his second season. After winning his first two races impressively, he was unlucky to be beaten in

Vaguely Noble returns to be unsaddled after his last race for Brook Holliday, when he won the Observer Gold Cup. Newmarket and its sales ring is the next stop.

The mission is accomplished as Vaguely Noble strides away from Sir Ivor to win the Prix de l'Arc de Triomphe.

the Grand Prix de Saint-Cloud but, reunited with his English-based Australian jockey Bill Williamson, he removed the blemish by winning his last two races.

The Arc was the climax, and faced by eight individual Classic winners, he stormed to the front two furlongs from home. The writing was on the wall for all but Sir Ivor, and though the Derby winner showed his customary acceleration, it was not enough to halt the relentless surge of Vaguely Noble, who was not hard pressed to win by three lengths.

The gamble had paid off and Vaguely Noble was retired to stud in the United States, though European observers wondered whether the unfashionably bred colt with middle-distance, grass-track form would be suited by American breeding conditions. They soon had their answer; Vaguely Noble's commanding presence, outstanding racing record and equable temperament, plus Hunt's support, brought a succession of able mares to his Kentucky quarters.

From the outset he proved himself as adept a sire as he had been a racehorse. In his first crop came Dahlia, twice winner of the King George VI and Queen Elizabeth Stakes, and by the time of his sudden death from a heart attack in April 1989 – with the winners of 29 European Group 1 races to his name – he had become one of the world's foremost sires.

Would he have run in the Arc, let alone won it, had he not been entered for the sales by his breeder's son? Would he have done so well at stud had it not been for Nelson Bunker Hunt's decision to take a share in him? No one can tell.

CAREER RECORD

Major race wins

1967 Observer Gold Cup

1968 Prix de Guiche, Prix du Lys, Prix de Chantilly, Prix de l'Arc de Triomphe

NIJINSKY

Born 1967. By Northern Dancer out of Flaming Page, by Bull Page.
Owned: Charles Engelhard. Trained: Vincent O'Brien, in Ireland.

Nijinsky is two-thirds of his way towards the Triple Crown, winning the Derby from Gyr and Stintino.

The first winner of the British Triple Crown of 2,000 Guineas, Derby and St Leger for 35 years, Nijinsky may also be the last for at least the same length of time. Defeats in his final two races, the Arc de Triomphe and the Champion Stakes, knocked some of the edge off his reputation, and part of the blame fell, unfairly, on the St Leger. The mud stuck, and the last, and longest, Classic is no longer an automatic target for a colt who has won the Guineas and the Derby.

Head and shoulders above the rest: that was Nijinsky, the first winner of the Triple Crown since Bahram in 1935.

Whether it was fair to blight Nijinsky for failing to fight back against Sassafras in the Arc after being asked to make up a lot of ground to get to the front, and for crying enough was enough in the Champion, is immaterial. There was no denying his outstanding achievements in victory.

Bought by the platinum king Charles Engelhard for a Canadian yearling record of $84,000, Nijinsky was Europe's top two-year-old, winning his five races with increasing authority. It was unthinkable that he would be beaten in the Guineas, and he was most impressive, but such were the doubts about his ability to stay a mile and a half in the Derby that for the first and only time in his life he started odds against. The doubts disappeared in the Epsom straight as Lester Piggott shook up Nijinsky and he surged past Gyr to win by two and a half lengths.

Nijinsky had less to do in winning the Irish Sweeps Derby, which he accomplished with ease, and then came the best impression of all, his summary dismissal of a good-class field for the King George VI and Queen Elizabeth Stakes. Nijinsky was

Lester Piggott and Nijinsky formed a perfect combination.

the only three-year-old in a six-horse line-up which included the previous year's Derby winner Blakeney; he crushed them, with Piggott easing him down as if it were a minor race in the provinces, not Britain's finest test of different generations.

Two statements sum up Nijinsky's career after being syndicated for stud in the United States at a world record valuation of $5.44 million. *Racehorses of 1970* said: 'Good racehorses don't always make good stallions but they have most things in their favour, and a really high-class one like Nijinsky all the more so.' And in January 1992, two months before Nijinsky's death, bloodstock expert Tony Morris wrote: 'He has generated more success, over a wider area, than any of the other truly great racehorses in the history of the Turf.'

Two Derby winners (Golden Fleece and Shahrastani), a French Derby winner (Caerleon), two British sires' championships and over 90 European Pattern wins illustrate his success as a sire in Europe; a Kentucky Derby winner (Ferdinand), three Breeders' Cup winners, and more than a hundred Graded stakes wins reveal his prowess in the States.

The complete thoroughbred: that was Nijinsky.

CAREER RECORD

Major race wins

1969 Railway Stakes, Anglesey Stakes, Beresford Stakes, Dewhurst Stakes

1970 Gladness Stakes, 2,000 Guineas Stakes, Derby Stakes, Irish Sweeps Derby, King George VI and Queen Elizabeth Stakes, St Leger Stakes

Brigadier Gerard

Born 1968. By Queen's Hussar out of La Paiva, by Prince Chevalier. Owned: Mrs Jean Hislop. Trained: Dick Hern.

Brigadier Gerard stands proud after beating Mill Reef in the 2,000 Guineas.

Outstanding horses come along so rarely that when two arrive in one generation, horseracing itself is the biggest winner. Brigadier Gerard was one of them, and Mill Reef the other. Together they shone throughout three seasons, and coming only a year after Nijinsky, they made this a golden era for British race fans.

Two horses so closely matched naturally divided opinion among public and professionals alike. Dan Sheppard, the Jockey Club handicapper, rated Mill Reef the better by 4lb in 1971, while *Timeform* had them locked at a rating of 141. The following year *Timeform* raised Brigadier Gerard to 144 and reckoned he was the equal of Tudor Minstrel and second only to Sea-Bird (by 1lb) in their post-war experience.

The Brigadier had everything but an unbeaten record – British breeding; well-established owners in Jean and John Hislop; a highly respected trainer in Dick Hern; a supreme stylist of a jockey in Joe Mercer; and to his own credit commanding good looks, speed, soundness and courage, the ability to win from five furlongs to a mile and a half, and 17 victories for more than £250,000.

Brigadier Gerard puts plenty of daylight between himself and Dictus in the Queen Elizabeth II Stakes (right), but Joe Mercer has to work harder before he beats Gold Rod and Home Guard in the Eclipse Stakes (below).

Brigadier Gerard holds the record for the number of wins in Pattern races at 13. Owners Jean and John Hislop are delighted after the first, in the 2,000 Guineas.

Even his one defeat – by the Derby winner Roberto in a hell-for-leather race for the Benson and Hedges Gold Cup – was such a surprise that it made no difference to his standing. And when he came back to win the Queen Elizabeth II Stakes in smashing style and the Champion Stakes in an emotional finale on his last two appearances, defeat at York was just a memory.

Brigadier Gerard met Mill Reef once, and beat him, by an imperious three lengths in the 2,000 Guineas. Thereafter, a combination of fate and circumstance kept them apart – The Brigadier was campaigned mainly at a mile or a mile and a quarter while his great rival for the public's affection raced over longer distances.

The Guineas success was undoubtedly one of Brigadier Gerard's best, but others stood out – his gallant fight to overcome a quagmire and Sparkler in the St James's Palace Stakes; his defeat of older horses in the Goodwood Mile; his disdainful treatment of the subsequent Irish Sweeps Derby winner Steel Pulse in the Prince of Wales's Stakes, and his courage in beating three Classic winners on the one occasion he ran a mile and a half, in the King George VI and Queen Elizabeth Stakes.

Hugely popular with race crowds and outstanding in ability, Brigadier Gerard sired winners of the St Leger (Light Cavalry) and Champion Stakes (Vayrann), but he died of a heart attack in November 1989, a relative failure at stud. It was enough that there was one Brigadier Gerard as a racehorse.

CAREER RECORD

Major/Group race wins

1970 Middle Park Stakes

1971 2,000 Guineas Stakes, St James's Palace Stakes, Sussex Stakes, Goodwood Mile, Queen Elizabeth II Stakes, Champion Stakes

1972 Lockinge Stakes, Westbury Stakes, Prince of Wales's Stakes, Eclipse Stakes, King George VI and Queen Elizabeth Stakes, Queen Elizabeth II Stakes, Champion Stakes

Mill Reef

Born 1968. By Never Bend out of Milan Mill, by Princequillo.
Owned: Paul Mellon. Trained: Ian Balding.

Comparisons may be odious, but the temptation to mention Mill Reef and Brigadier Gerard in the same conversation is never far away. The fact that the two great rivals never met again after the 2,000 Guineas merely added fuel to contemporary arguments.

From the day he toyed with the odds-on Fireside Chat on his debut, Mill Reef made news, whether on the track or off it. They even made a film and a long-playing record about his life and times, subtitled 'Something to brighten the morning'.

It was not simply the mornings that Mill Reef brightened; he shone on a succession of afternoons: in the York mud as a two-year-old, when he pulled himself ten lengths clear of the rest in the Gimcrack Stakes; in the glory of Britain's three major summer contests, the Derby, Eclipse and King George VI and Queen Elizabeth Stakes; and in the white heat of competition in the Prix de l'Arc de Triomphe.

Bred by his owner in the United States, Mill Reef wasted no time in signalling his prowess. He won the Coventry Stakes at Royal Ascot by eight lengths, and after York notched two more wins. The only reason he did not top the two-year-old Free Handicap was because of his single, narrow, midsummer defeat at the hands of My Swallow in France.

Mill Reef reversed placings with My Swallow in the Guineas but did not have the reserves to cope with Brigadier Gerard. That was the last time Mill Reef was beaten.

He dispelled doubts about his stamina in the Derby, wearing down the resolute

Linden Tree to win by two lengths; he put the best older horses firmly in their place in the Eclipse Stakes and the King George VI and Queen Elizabeth Stakes; and he ended his second season as the undisputed mile-and-a-half champion of Europe with a course record victory on firm ground in the Arc.

The stage was set for a sizzling 1972 and, best of all, a possible rematch between the two giants. Mill Reef whetted the appetite with an astonishing win in the Prix Ganay, where he made ten second-raters look fifth rate, and he kept up the interest in the Coronation Cup. Then, disaster struck.

Mill Reef was below par and missed the Eclipse and King George, both won by Brigadier Gerard, and a niggling injury kept him out of the Benson and Hedges Gold Cup, which The Brigadier lost. Just two days after, it was announced that Mill Reef would be kept in training as a five-year-old, and while he was being prepared for a pre-Arc outing, he badly fractured his near foreleg on the gallops.

No one can doubt Mill Reef's stamina after he wins the Derby from Linden Tree. Irish Ball, from France, is third, and Lombardo (second right), from Ireland, fourth.

All smiles as Mill Reef and Geoff Lewis make their way into the winner's circle after the Derby.

Mill Reef's trainer Ian Balding (left) and owner Paul Mellon admire the bronze tribute to their champion at the Kingsclere stables.

A complicated and costly operation saved Mill Reef's life, and the attention of Ian Balding's staff and the colt's own patience enabled him to start a new career at the National Stud. The value of that care and devotion is immense, for after a stuttering start he emerged as the premier British-based stallion of the last 15 years.

Twice champion sire – including the year after his death in early 1986 – he is responsible for two Derby winners (Shirley Heights and Reference Point), as well as winners of the 2,000 Guineas (Doyoun) and French Derby (Acamas), and the six-times Group 1 winner Glint of Gold. This is one comparison with Brigadier Gerard in which Mill Reef wins hands down, no argument.

CAREER RECORD

Major/Group race wins

1970 Coventry Stakes, Gimcrack Stakes, Imperial Stakes, Dewhurst Stakes

1971 Greenham Stakes, Derby Stakes, Eclipse Stakes, King George VI and Queen Elizabeth Stakes, Prix de l'Arc de Triomphe

1972 Prix Ganay, Coronation Cup

Allez France

Born 1970. By Sea-Bird out of Priceless Gem, by Hail to Reason. Owned: Daniel Wildenstein. Trained: Albert Klimscha; Angel Penna, in France.

Success does not always receive its just rewards. Allez France met Dahlia six times and finished in front of her on every occasion, yet Dahlia retired with world-record earnings for a filly. Allez France counted some of the best performances by a filly in the last 40 years among her 13 victories, yet racegoers in Britain and the United States never saw her at her best. And while Allez France was peerless on the racecourse, she was an intermittent and unsuccessful broodmare.

In all other respects Allez France could not be faulted. She was impeccably bred, being by the great Sea-Bird out of a top-class and well-related racemare who fetched a world-record $395,000 in 1970. She was magnificently imposing in appearance, had terrific acceleration and a marvellous temperament, showed her form on most types of going, and stayed at the top from two years old to five.

Bought privately in the United States as a yearling for $160,000, she recouped her purchase price six times over, but the pleasure she gave her connections and those who followed her career from the grandstands, especially in France, could not be counted in cash terms.

From the outset she was a star, winning her only two races as a juvenile in most impressive fashion and proving her quality among her own sex as a three-year-old with wins in the Poule d'Essai des Pouliches (French 1,000 Guineas), Prix de Diane (French Oaks) and Prix Vermeille. Only the English-trained four-year-old colt Rheingold beat her in the Prix de l'Arc de Triomphe that year.

Trainer Angel Penna keeps an eye on Allez France as she prepares for exercise at Chantilly.

Allez France, the Queen of Paris, and Yves Saint-Martin parade at Longchamp, where she gained 12 of her 13 successes.

Allez France's subsequent defeat by Hurry Harriet in the 1973 Champion Stakes was inexplicable, made all the more perplexing by her achievements the following year, when arguably she was at her peak.

She was unbeaten in five races in 1974, when Penna took over her training from the retired Klimscha. She twice rubbed Dahlia's nose in the dirt at Longchamp, in the Prix d'Harcourt and Prix Ganay; she accomplished an awesome task set her by Yves Saint-Martin in the nine-furlong Prix d'Ispahan; and after a summer break she collected a prep race for the Prix de l'Arc de Triomphe before holding off Comtesse de Loir by a head in the real thing.

If Allez France was not quite so good at five years as she had been at four, so be it, but it still took until the autumn before she was dethroned. Even then, excuses of bad luck in running were advanced for her finishing only fifth behind Star Appeal in attempting an Arc double.

The fact had to be faced, however unpalatable it was, that Allez France could no longer dominate, and though she reversed placings with Star Appeal in the Champion Stakes, she could not cope with another filly, Rose Bowl. For the second time British racegoers had seen less than the best of Allez France. Sadly, the Americans saw even worse, for when she was sent to race at Santa Anita in November, she finished last of 11 on dirt.

To be beaten on her last two appearances was an anti-climax; at least for the French, who adored her, it had happened out of sight.

CAREER RECORD

Group race wins

1972 Criterium des Pouliches

1973 Poule d'Essai des Pouliches, Prix de Diane, Prix Vermeille

1974 Prix d'Harcourt, Prix Ganay, Prix d'Ispahan, Prix Foy, Prix de l'Arc de Triomphe

1975 Prix Ganay, Prix d'Ispahan, Prix Foy

Secretariat

Born 1970. By Bold Ruler out of Somethingroyal, by Princequillo. Owned: Meadow Stable. Trained: Lucien Laurin.

Horse of the Century, the greatest American champion, even Athlete of the Year: they were all ascribed to Secretariat, otherwise known throughout the United States as Big Red on account of his giant physique and bright chestnut colouring. He was a horse who became a national hero.

Only Man o' War was compared to Secretariat, and his supporters were won

Secretariat was hailed as the perfect racing machine.

over as soon as the Triple Crown fell for the first time in 25 years. When both Seattle Slew and Affirmed annexed the coveted treble in the next five years, no one considered it a slight on Secretariat; quite the opposite, since Secretariat achieved things neither of his juniors could accomplish. He won the Kentucky Derby in record time; he would have done the same in the Preakness Stakes had the track's timing equipment been in perfect working order, and he won the Belmont Stakes by 31 lengths, also in record time.

If the Triple Crown made up the winning hand for Secretariat, the Belmont Stakes was the ace. His was a performance of awesome power as he surged to the front in the first furlong and proceeded to gallop and gallop. Relentlessly he pulled farther away from his field, whom he had beaten into submission by halfway. More than a furlong after the winning post, jockey Ron Turcotte was still trying to pull up, and as the clock ticked on, Secretariat registered a world record for 13 furlongs, though he had been obliged to run only 12!

Veteran trainer Woody Stephens, who won the Belmont five times, was heard to reflect, 'I wouldn't have won one if I'd had to run against him,' before he summed up Secretariat in a word, 'Perfect. I have never seen a horse run the way he ran when he won the Belmont. To me that was perfection.'

Perfect breeding, perfect conformation, perfect temperament: Secretariat had them all. More importantly, he had the perfect racing engine. It was not necessarily built for blinding acceleration, but it cruised at a higher speed than the rest.

Secretariat was not invincible. He lost on his first appearance, where he was caught flat-footed at the start of the race and was hampered during it. He was beaten into third place in his Derby prep race. He was skinned by an average racer called Onion at Saratoga, and he went down on two other occasions. But each time he bounced back.

So well did he recover from his debut defeat that he won his remaining seven races as a two-year-old and was named Horse of the Year, a rare tribute for a juvenile. So far, so good, but when he was syndicated in February 1974 – for a world-record $6.08 million – to pay inheritance taxes, it meant those investors who risked $190,000 a share were gambling on his winning the Triple Crown. Anything less and he would not have been worth the money.

The future looked less than rosy when Secretariat was beaten into third place in the Wood Memorial Stakes, but the Kentucky Derby was less than two months away, and the rest is history.

They broke one of the moulds when Secretariat was created, so it was no surprise that his stud career was something of an anti-climax. Still, he was far from a failure, witness a Horse of the Year (Lady's Secret), a dual Classic winner (Risen Star) and a Canadian champion (Medaille d'Or) among the list of credits before his death in October 1989, the result of laminitis.

Secretariat's name will linger in international pedigrees for many a year; his racing performances will last as long as there are people around with memories.

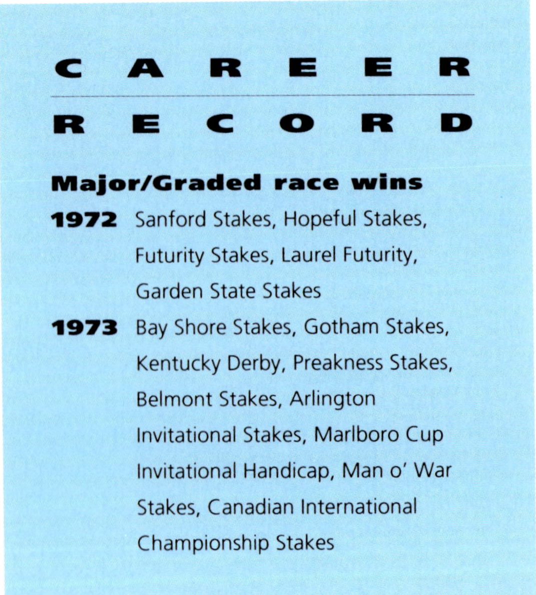

CAREER RECORD

Major/Graded race wins

1972 Sanford Stakes, Hopeful Stakes, Futurity Stakes, Laurel Futurity, Garden State Stakes

1973 Bay Shore Stakes, Gotham Stakes, Kentucky Derby, Preakness Stakes, Belmont Stakes, Arlington Invitational Stakes, Marlboro Cup Invitational Handicap, Man o' War Stakes, Canadian International Championship Stakes

GRUNDY

Born 1972. By Great Nephew out of Word From Lundy, by Worden.
Owned: Carlo Vittadini. Trained: Peter Walwyn.

Out of sight, out of mind: the saying might have been made for Grundy, whose export from the National Stud to Japan in 1983 left us with only memories, and fast-receding ones at that.

Yet Grundy deserves to be remembered, and not only for his flashy looks. The light-coloured chestnut with flaxen tail and mane beat Mill Reef's record for career earnings by a horse trained in Britain; he was voted Racehorse of the Year in 1975; and the Jockey Club handicapper had him top of the list at both two and three years.

Those were the measures of his achievements; the manner was as bright as his appearance.

One race will always stand out, and when arguments begin about the Race of the Century – or any other collection of years – Grundy versus Bustino for the King George VI and Queen Elizabeth Diamond Stakes will have a permanent place among the candidates. But Grundy was no one-race wonder.

He began on a high note, bearing out his home reputation by winning a newcomers' race at Ascot in July, and got better and better. By the end of his first season he had worked his way to the top via the

Grundy is much too good for the filly Nobiliary at Epsom, and it's on to Ireland for the Derby double. His duel with Bustino is just around the corner.

Pat Eddery and Grundy return in triumph after their battle with Bustino.

Champagne Stakes at Doncaster and the Dewhurst Stakes at Newmarket.

At the end of 1974 it would have taken a brave man to forecast that Grundy would be beaten in the 2,000 Guineas, and a fool to suggest he would be beaten in the Greenham Stakes beforehand. But those who thought they knew best were reckoning without the unexpected – a kick in the face from a stablemate, and the arrival of an unknown quantity from Italy.

Unwelcome attention on the gallops resulted in Grundy's missing training, and he was beaten at Newbury by lack of fitness, arduous ground conditions and a useful opponent in Mark Anthony. There were no excuses in the Guineas; Grundy was simply beaten on the day by a better horse at the distance, the one-time Italian-trained Bolkonski. Considering that Grundy was also Italian owned, the irony of his Classic defeat was obvious.

However, the Guineas was Grundy's last reverse until his King George exertions took their toll in the Benson and Hedges Gold Cup at York. In between he strolled away with the Irish 2,000 Guineas (with Mark Anthony third), he won the Derby in great style and completed the double in Ireland, and he defeated Bustino in a pulsating battle at Ascot.

In terms of pure ability the Derby was arguably Grundy's finest hour, even allowing that his chief rival Green Dancer ran below his best. On the balance of three-year-old form Green Dancer needed to be better than his best to beat Grundy that day, for having held a handy place throughout, Grundy and Pat Eddery had everything under control from a long way out.

Elements of regret emerged through the later stages of Grundy's career, ranging from the decision to bypass the Prix de l'Arc de Triomphe, through his defeat at York and his moderate achievements at stud, and ending with his departure to the obscurity of Japan. But no one could take away his Derby glory, and no one can forget his tussle with Bustino.

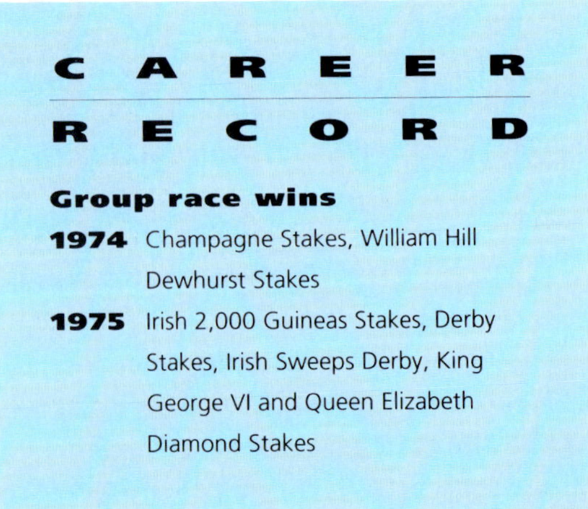

CAREER RECORD

Group race wins

1974 Champagne Stakes, William Hill Dewhurst Stakes

1975 Irish 2,000 Guineas Stakes, Derby Stakes, Irish Sweeps Derby, King George VI and Queen Elizabeth Diamond Stakes

ALLEGED

Born 1974. By Hoist the Flag out of Princess Pout, by Prince John.
Owned: Robert Fluor and Robert Sangster.
Trained: Vincent O'Brien, in Ireland.

Autumn comes and Alleged is back at his best to complete an Arc de Triomphe double.

Time was of the essence for Alleged. Its influence could be seen in the way his valuation rocketed – from $40,000 as a yearling, which 'pinhooker' Monty Roberts paid his breeder; to $175,000 as a two-year-old, which agent Billy Macdonald paid on behalf of partners Robert Fluor and Robert Sangster; to £1 million, which Sangster paid for all but 5 per cent of Fluor's share in 1977; to $3.5 million for a half-share, which John Gaines offered and was refused later in 1977; to $16 million, his final syndication price in 1978.

And it was time which enabled Alleged to show his worth on the racecourse, where he won all but one of his ten races and became only the third horse since the Second World War to win the Prix de l'Arc

Alleged and Lester Piggott play to a packed audience, powering home to win their first Prix de l'Arc de Triomphe.

de Triomphe twice. The others were Tantieme and Ribot in the 1950s.

Alleged was an unprepossessing yearling who was straightened out by Roberts, a renowned horseman who later became well known in Britain for his ability to educate young horses with the minimum fuss and in a remarkably short time. And as a new horse in training with Vincent O'Brien, Alleged was way down the pecking order. Even after winning his two-year-old debut race by eight lengths, the likes of The Minstrel, Godswalk and Be My Guest had far higher profiles.

Alleged won his first race as a three-year-old; two weeks later he won his second,

where he was O'Brien's third string and started at 33–1 to his stablemates' 5–4 and 4–1. But still O'Brien took his time and Alleged had the summer off. When he returned, in the Great Voltigeur Stakes at York, it was obvious that the real Alleged had arrived, for he stormed at least eight lengths clear of a high-class field, which included several who had run with credit in the Epsom and Irish Derbys.

The surprises were not yet finished, for Alleged, the new-found revelation, was beaten in the St Leger, where on the day and over the distance he found the Queen's filly Dunfermline too good. But back to a mile and a half in the Prix de l'Arc de Triomphe, that defeat was avenged and Alleged reached the pinnacle, taking the lead after three furlongs and powering his way to a length-and-a-half victory.

A temporary ban on imports to the United States ensured that Alleged remained in Ireland as a four-year-old, though with so little racing and so much time on his side, he would probably have stayed in training whatever the circumstances. For the third year in a row it was autumn before he was ready to do his best, and for the second year it was the Arc de Triomphe which beckoned. In the first three from the start, Alleged was going like a winner as the field turned for home and his turn of foot settled matters in a few strides.

At stud in the States it took Alleged a couple of years to produce offspring out of the top drawer – the first being Law Society, whom O'Brien trained to win the Irish Derby. Since then he has established himself in the highest league of stallions with such as Sir Harry Lewis (Irish Derby), Hours After (French Derby), Midway Lady (1,000 Guineas and Oaks) and Miss Alleged (Breeders' Cup Turf). Almost without exception the best of his produce take after their sire – they need time and patience.

CAREER RECORD

Group race wins

1977 Royal Whip Stakes, Gallinule Stakes, Great Voltigeur Stakes, Prix de l'Arc de Triomphe

1978 Royal Whip Stakes, Prix du Prince d'Orange, Prix de l'Arc de Triomphe

TROY

Born 1976. By Petingo out of La Milo, by Hornbeam.
Owned: Sir Michael Sobell and Sir Arnold Weinstock.
Trained: Dick Hern.

Derby Day 200, and Troy's joint-owner Sir Michael Sobell receives the race trophy.

Within the space of three months in 1983 the two colts who gave new meaning to the winning distance in the Derby were gone. Shergar, successful by the record margin of ten lengths in 1981, was spirited away from his quarters in Ireland, and Troy, seven-length winner two years previously, died of a perforated gut. The mysterious circumstances of Shergar's disappearance have ensured him lasting fame beyond the mere confines of horseracing; of Troy there are only words and pictures on a page to remind us of his achievements.

Derby Day 1979 was the peak of Troy's career. He had won races before, and he was to win three races afterwards, but he was never better than at Epsom for the two-hundredth running of the Derby.

There, he was one of three runners from the Dick Hern stable in an unusually large field of 23, which could be explained by the open nature of the race rather than by its historical significance. At the finish there was only one in it, with Troy galloping up the centre of the course well clear. That, however, is only part of the story, for two furlongs out Troy was ninth.

His jockey Willie Carson had elected to stay on the rail running down Tattenham Hill, and it was not until the field straightened for home that he began to move outside. Even when he was at last confronted by daylight, Troy had lengths to make up on the leader, but so fast was he

Troy dances away from his Derby rivals, winning by seven lengths from Dickens Hill.

travelling that the race was over a furlong out, and from that point Troy went farther and farther ahead.

The Derby vanquished were not slow coaches; Troy simply made them look so.

He proved nothing that was not already apparent by winning the Irish Sweeps Derby and the King George VI and Queen Elizabeth Diamond Stakes, and then, rather surprisingly, was brought back in distance for the Benson and Hedges Gold Cup as part of his preparation for the Prix de l'Arc de Triomphe. Roberto had accomplished the Epsom–York double seven years earlier – but unexpectedly, at the expense of the unbeaten Brigadier Gerard.

From the early stages of his career Troy had given every appearance of being a stayer. His wins as a two-year-old were over seven furlongs, and his two pre-Derby races were over ten and twelve furlongs. Returning to an extended mile and a quarter at York seemed an unusual step, but Troy took it in his stride, though he had a harder race than his odds of 1–2 might have suggested. Sadly, it was probably too hard a race, and Troy was beaten into third place in the Arc.

Winner of European record earnings in excess of £450,000, Troy was syndicated for £7.2 million (another European record) to stand at stud in Britain, where he completed three seasons and had started another before his untimely death. Fate had made sure that Troy would be judged on his dazzling Derby performance.

CAREER RECORD

Group race wins

1979 Classic Trial Stakes (Sandown Park), Derby Stakes, Irish Sweeps Derby, King George VI and Queen Elizabeth Diamond Stakes, Benson and Hedges Gold Cup

Shergar

Born 1978. By Great Nephew out of Sharmeen, by Val de Loir. Owned: HH Aga Khan. Trained: Michael Stoute.

A champion in his slower paces. Shergar and Walter Swinburn go to post for the King George VI and Queen Elizabeth Diamond Stakes.

Shergar was known beyond the narrow confines of the horse-racing world even before his mysterious disappearance from the Ballymany Stud in Ireland on the night of 8 February 1983. After it, he took on the mantle of a world celebrity, becoming the subject of national newspaper stories, books and a television drama-documentary.

None of the millions of words consumed by his pursuers unequivocally answered the question about his fate. There were many theories, some fanciful and others more reasonable, and most centred on the conclusion that he was taken by the IRA.

Shergar's owner-breeder, the Aga Khan – who held six shares in the syndicate which owned him at the time of his disappearance – was reported in 1989 as saying: 'The plain fact is that Shergar was kidnapped by a wing of the IRA. It may well have been a unilateral decision by these people, not approved by the leadership. It most certainly backfired on them.'

Shergar turns the Derby into a procession, and strolls home ten lengths in front of Glint of Gold and Scintillating Air. The rest are almost impossible to spot.

That, for the moment and perhaps for all time, is as near as anyone will get to a public explanation. Shergar seems destined to remain the Lord Lucan of the racing game.

Shergar left a single set of foals to represent him; it was nowhere near enough to judge how successful he might have been as a stallion. Rather he will be remembered for his racecourse exploits, which were outstanding and had already projected him beyond the racing pages.

He might not have figured prominently in his stable's early two-year-old plans, but by the end of his first season he had blossomed into a leading candidate for three-year-old honours after winning a small race on his debut and finishing second in Group 1 class on his only other outing.

Even during the winter he was among the 33–1 shots for the Derby, but by the day of the race he was a certainty and started at 11–10 on, the shortest-priced favourite for the Epsom Classic since Sir Ivor in 1968. His standing rested on the evidence of his own progress, after winning a Sandown trial by a devastating ten lengths and the Chester Vase by 12 lengths, and the apparent lack of worthwhile opposition. Unusually, there was a Derby winner in the field – Glint of Gold, who had won the Italian equivalent – but there were only two French runners (and one of them refused to start) and none from Ireland.

Betting on the Derby was lopsided, and so too was the result. Racing two horses off the rail on the run round Tattenham Corner, Shergar was cantering upside the leaders and once he was eased to the front early in the straight, there was only one horse that mattered. Shergar raced clear in a matter of

Shergar's lad Dickie McCabe and Michael Stoute's travelling head lad Jimmy Scott didn't know it at the time, but his appearance in the St Leger was to be the great colt's last on a racecourse.

strides with a blistering display of acceleration. At the winning post he was ten lengths ahead of runner-up Glint of Gold, and only five horses in the field of 17 came within 20 lengths of him.

Walter Swinburn, Shergar's 19-year-old jockey, was suspended for the Irish Sweeps Derby, and Lester Piggott deputized in an unchallenged success. Swinburn was back for the rest of the season, which brought another decisive victory in the King George VI and Queen Elizabeth Diamond Stakes and a surprising defeat into fourth place in the St Leger.

Shergar never ran again, and his retirement before the Prix de l'Arc de Triomphe was a source of some criticism by those professionals who felt his owner had ducked the issue. Sadly, the economics of putting his reputation on the line after being syndicated during the summer for £10 million – a record for a stallion to stand in Europe – proved too great, and he left the scene richer for his exploits but after only eight public appearances.

CAREER RECORD

Group race wins

1981 Guardian Newspaper Classic Trial, Chester Vase, Derby Stakes, Irish Sweeps Derby, King George VI and Queen Elizabeth Diamond Stakes

Dancing Brave

Born 1983. By Lyphard out of Navajo Princess, by Drone.
Owned: Khalid Abdullah. Trained: Guy Harwood.

Dancing Brave (left) turns the Derby tables on Shahrastani (white blaze) as he wins the King George VI and Queen Elizabeth Diamond Stakes from Shardari and Triptych.

When Dancing Brave was sold to Japan early in 1992, hardly a word of regret was heard. His fall from favour was remarkably complete, influenced wholly by the passage of time and his failure to make an instant mark as a sire. Yet only two years earlier he had been voted Horse of the Decade in a newspaper poll.

The accolade was deserved. It was also virtually inevitable that it would come his way, since the leading European handicappers rated him the best horse to have raced since they began compiling the International Classifications in 1977.

Dancing Brave tops their order of merit

There's no stopping Dancing Brave, who races through to beat Bering in the Prix de l'Arc de Triomphe.

with a rating of 141, 1lb above both Alleged and Shergar and 3lb in front of El Gran Senor. His domination in 1986 was such that he ranked 7lb ahead of his nearest rivals, Bering and Shahrastani, winners between them of the English, Irish and French Derbys.

The fact that Dancing Brave did not win a Derby, particularly *the* Derby at Epsom, will rankle with his supporters as long as they draw breath, and why he did not win the Derby will remain a topic of discussion and argument for as long as any two people who saw the race are around to talk about it.

Greatly exaggerated waiting tactics employed by his jockey Greville Starkey and failure to adapt to the unique Epsom course combined to put Dancing Brave in an impossible position early in the straight; and though he finished with a flourish, he was beaten half a length into second place behind Shahrastani.

The European handicappers' view of their respective merits was illustrated by the

Professionals criticized Dancing Brave for his make and shape – and his parrot mouth – but no one doubted his racing talents.

International Classification, and the Derby was the one race where Dancing Brave's brilliant acceleration did not pay dividends. His only other defeat in a total of ten races came on his swansong, in the Breeders' Cup Turf at Santa Anita, where his turn of foot was never apparent.

Prior to the Derby, Dancing Brave had shown his class by winning the 2,000 Guineas over a mile by three lengths. After it, he put his middle-distance record into proper perspective with a four-length win over the tough French filly Triptych in the Eclipse Stakes and a reputation-restoring victory over Shahrastani (who ran below form) in the King George VI and Queen Elizabeth Diamond Stakes.

Each time Dancing Brave's success was built on a calm temperament and exciting finishing speed, two attributes which brought him his finest hour in Paris in October, when, with Abdullah's new retained jockey Pat Eddery in the saddle, he raced home in record time to beat a high-class field headed by Bering. Sweeping through on the wide outside, Dancing Brave was, in a word, brilliant. If only he could have done the same in the Derby ...

CAREER RECORD

Group race wins

1986 Charles Heidsieck Champagne Craven Stakes, General Accident 2,000 Guineas Stakes, King George VI and Queen Elizabeth Diamond Stakes, Scottish Equitable Select Stakes, Trusthouse Forte Prix de l'Arc de Triomphe

Reference Point

Born 1984. By Mill Reef out of Home on the Range, by Habitat. Owned: Louis Freedman. Trained: Henry Cecil.

At a time when large-scale British-based owner-breeders were becoming an endangered species, along came Reference Point to give the dwindling band a boost. He could not be expected to turn the tide single-handed, but he did provide a much needed reminder that success does not always have to be bought.

When Reference Point emerged, Louis Freedman had been in racing for 20 years, building on his purchase of Lord Astor's Cliveden Stud to such purpose that his yellow-and-black racing colours had been carried by several useful racers, mostly

Steve Cauthen uses Reference Point's strong gallop to the full and wins the Derby from Most Welcome (noseband) and Bellotto.

Tattenham Corner is the turning-point of the Derby as Reference Point starts to accelerate away from his rivals. The group on his heels includes Most Welcome (noseband), Ascot Knight, Ibn Bey (rails) and Ajdal (almost hidden).

fillies. None was in the same class as Reference Point; indeed, few horses at any time in the last 25 years have been his match.

The official handicappers rated Reference Point at 135, the equal of Blushing Groom, Ile de Bourbon, Slip Anchor, Teenoso and The Minstrel, and inferior to a group of six headed by Dancing Brave on 141. *Timeform* regarded him more highly, giving him a rating of 139 to rank behind only Sea-Bird, Brigadier Gerard, Ribot, Mill Reef, Dancing Brave, Shergar and Vaguely Noble among middle-distance horses of the last 40 years.

The comparisons can be argued about, but there is no doubting that Reference Point dominated his generation, and this is the evidence on which he can be regarded as outstanding.

Reference Point dominated in ability and performance, for his racing style involved being sent off in front. He usually stayed there. Apart from his first race – where he finished third – and his last, in the Prix de l'Arc de Triomphe – where he ran way below his best and might have been feeling a slight injury – only Mtoto ever headed him on the racecourse, and even then he had to show improved form to beat Reference Point in the Eclipse Stakes.

Even the best jockeys can make occasional mistakes in their assessment of horses, and Steve Cauthen did just that about Reference Point when he preferred to ride Suhailie for Henry Cecil in the William Hill Futurity, Britain's top mile race for two-year-olds. Cauthen could hardly have been more wrong, for while Suhailie trailed in seventh of ten, Pat Eddery and Reference

Louis Freedman achieves every owner's dream, leading in Reference Point after the Derby.

Point galloped away to win by an official margin of five lengths which looked more like seven on the photo-finish print.

On this evidence Reference Point was the best two-year-old of the year, and unlike other claimants from around that time, he stayed on top as a three-year-old. There was a setback when a sinus operation delayed his reappearance and he was not fully fit when he won the Mecca-Dante Stakes in mid-May, but he started a hot favourite for the Derby and led from pillar to post.

His strong galloping style was not entirely suited by Epsom's undulations, but Ascot, for the King George VI and Queen Elizabeth Diamond Stakes, provided exactly the right test and he came into his own. A high-class field turned out for Britain's premier middle-distance race but they were quickly forced into submission by Reference Point's exhilarating pace. His speed might not have been as instant as that of Shergar or Dancing Brave, but it was of the highest order and though he later won the Great Voltigeur Stakes and St Leger, the King George VI remains the high spot of his career and the yardstick against which he should be measured.

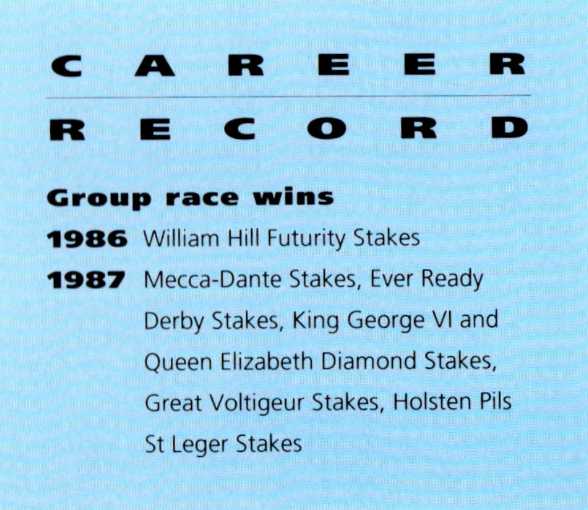

CAREER RECORD

Group race wins

1986 William Hill Futurity Stakes

1987 Mecca-Dante Stakes, Ever Ready Derby Stakes, King George VI and Queen Elizabeth Diamond Stakes, Great Voltigeur Stakes, Holsten Pils St Leger Stakes

Nashwan

Born 1986. By Blushing Groom out of Height of Fashion, by Bustino. Owned: Hamdan Al-Maktoum. Trained: Neil Graham; Dick Hern.

Nashwan was not the best three-year-old racing in 1989; he was not even the second-best, according to those whose job it is to produce figures showing comparative merit. Yet he was the public favourite, and retired with one statistic that was his alone, and may remain so for some time.

End-of-season merit tables published by the official handicappers and *Timeform* had Old Vic, winner of the French and Irish Derbys, and the outstanding miler Zilzal ahead of Nashwan. The officials bracketed them on 134, 3lb in front of Nashwan, while the well-respected private company went down in 1lb steps from Zilzal's 137 to Old Vic and Nashwan.

As matters of fact these are probably

Sporting the Nashwan colours, his lad Alan Thimbleby has every reason to be delighted after the King George VI and Queen Elizabeth Diamond Stakes.

Nashwan and Willie Carson take the straight route to victory in the Derby, winning by five lengths from Terimon (centre), with the obscured Cacoethes third.

1

Cacoethes (right) gives Nashwan a much harder race in the King George VI and Queen Elizabeth Diamond Stakes than at Epsom, but the result is the same.

correct interpretations, but as long as racing is bound up in expression of opinion, there will always be room for other considerations. Here, Nashwan's supporters will point to the reported comments of trainer Dick Hern – who was ill during Nashwan's first season when his assistant Neil Graham held the licence – and jockey Willie Carson, both of whom regarded Nashwan as the best horse they had been associated with.

Again, that's as maybe, but there is another measure of Nashwan's greatness, tied in with the assertion of Hern about his two undisputed champions, that Troy would not have won the 2,000 Guineas and Brigadier Gerard might not have won the Derby. Nashwan did more than win both; he also won the Eclipse Stakes and King George VI and Queen Elizabeth Diamond Stakes, and was the first horse ever to claim all four Group 1 races in one season. Such an achievement required versatility, courage, determination and class. Nashwan had all four, wrapped up in a huge frame and powered along by a smooth, long-striding action.

Two wins from as many races as a two-year-old suggested Nashwan was a rising star, but they were not gained in the best company and Hern had others with higher claims. Only a month before the Guineas Nashwan could be backed at 40–1, but so swiftly did confidence in him grow that on the day, without having been on a racecourse again, he was favourite for both Newmarket (3–1) and Epsom (2–1). He justified both positions, winning the Guineas in the fastest electrically recorded time and the Derby by five lengths – with a devastating display over the last two furlongs.

In the Eclipse, Nashwan's main rivals – Warning and Indian Skimmer – ran below their best, but there was no stopping the big chestnut colt. A fortnight later he had to battle his hardest to beat Cacoethes in the King George VI, but he was nothing if not gallant and the elusive big-race fourtimer was his. Though unsuspected at the time, it was also his last success.

There was never much chance of Nashwan's remaining in training as a four-year-old but it was hoped he might be allowed to add to his glory by tackling the missing piece in the Triple Crown, the St Leger. His trainer was in favour but his owner was not, and so the Prix de l'Arc de Triomphe became his final target. He was destined not to reach it, for he flopped badly in a preparation race at Longchamp and was eventually taken out of both the Arc and Champion Stakes, and out of training.

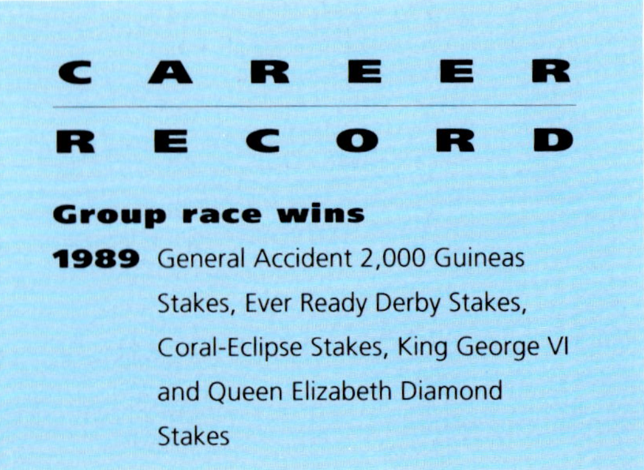

CAREER RECORD

Group race wins

1989 General Accident 2,000 Guineas Stakes, Ever Ready Derby Stakes, Coral-Eclipse Stakes, King George VI and Queen Elizabeth Diamond Stakes

Dayjur

Born 1987. By Danzig out of Gold Beauty, by Mr Prospector.
Owned: Hamdan Al-Maktoum. Trained: Dick Hern.

Dayjur takes a flying leap to defeat by Safely Kept in the Breeders' Cup Sprint. Willie Carson does well to stay in the saddle but the victory they deserved has gone.

Fashion stalks the horseracing world just as stealthily as it does the catwalk; sometimes a trend is in, sometimes it is out. Over the last 25 years sprinters definitely come into the second category. Yet there is always room for an exception, and Dayjur was it.

It took until the middle of his second season, on his seventh appearance, to appreciate just how good a sprinter he was, but once he had put down his marker in the King's Stand Stakes at Royal Ascot, nothing in Europe could get to him.

From the start at Ascot he produced a scorching gallop which burnt off the opposition by halfway, and these forcing tactics came to be his trademark. Over five furlongs it resulted in a six-length win in the King's Stand Stakes and a course record in the Nunthorpe Stakes at York. Over six furlongs in the Ladbroke Sprint Cup it took him to a five-length advantage at the distance that was good enough to hold Royal Academy's late rally. And back to five furlongs in the Prix de l'Abbaye de Longchamp, it propelled him to a place in the record books as the first to win this group of four races.

Success in the Abbaye was not achieved without a moment of anxiety, for Dayjur shied at a railside advertising hoarding about a furlong from the finish and lost his

Dayjur has the power, and soon he will gain the glory of winning the Ladbroke Sprint Cup from Royal Academy.

rhythm for a stride or two. At the time the incident seemed to be of little significance; within three weeks it had become an omen.

When Dayjur was returned to his native United States for the Breeders' Cup Sprint at New York's Belmont Park, he had the odds stacked against him. He was racing on dirt, he was running round a bend for the first time, and he was taking on the Americans at their own helter-skelter sprint game. And all this at the end of a long season, after a transatlantic trip into unknown territory in more ways than a few.

Despite the drawbacks Dayjur started favourite, and it was no fault of anyone but Dayjur that he did not win. Pushed along from the start to hold his place, he drew away with Safely Kept round the home turn and they battled head to head to the finish. Dayjur had just got his nose in front for what seemed the decisive move when, 50 yards from the finish, he leapt a shadow across the track. Carson brilliantly kept his seat, but the damage had been done and Dayjur – who amazingly took off again as they crossed the winning line – was beaten by a neck.

'We definitely had the best horse but sadly we don't get the money,' said a disconsolate Carson. But Dayjur did get the credit and when the International Classifications were published, he headed the list, regarded as the best horse to race in Europe in 1990.

For only the second time since the Classifications were introduced in 1977 a sprinter was top, Moorestyle in 1980 being the first. In other years sprinters have struggled to stay in touch with their middle-distance cousins, the best of them lagging between 2lb and 15lb behind the highest-rated horse. But Dayjur was the exception, and his rating of 133 made him the equal of Gentilhombre in 1977 as the best sprinter of the period. Some would say Dayjur was out on his own.

CAREER RECORD

Group race wins

1990 Sears Temple Stakes, King's Stand Stakes, Keeneland Nunthorpe Stakes, Ladbroke Sprint Cup Stakes, Ciga Prix de l'Abbaye de Longchamp

GENEROUS

Born 1988. By Caerleon out of Doff the Derby, by Master Derby. Owned: Fahd Salman. Trained: Paul Cole.

It often takes two horses to make a champion, and in 1991 Generous had a perfect foil in Suave Dancer. They met just twice, with the score at one-all, but so convincing was Generous in winning the Irish Derby – and so comprehensive, so inexplicable, was his defeat in the Prix de l'Arc de Triomphe – that only the most blinkered Suave Dancer supporter would argue about which was the better.

Europe's leading official handicappers had no doubt – at least not when they published their International Classifications, which placed British-based Generous on a rating of 137 and French-trained Suave Dancer on 136. The rumour goes that the French officials began the round-table discussions on the three-year-old Classification hoping to beat a different drum, but weight of argument forced them to back down.

The telling factor was the Irish Derby, where two colts, each with his local Derby in the bag, met at the peak of their form in a truly run race on perfect ground. Conditions were ideal for making comparisons, and Generous won by three lengths from Suave Dancer.

The big two frightened away all but four rivals and they dominated the race. Generous led after four furlongs; Suave Dancer stayed within striking distance and put in his challenge halfway up the straight, but Generous was simply too good for him.

Generous can look forward to continuing attention as he starts his stallion career at Banstead Manor Stud.

Generous had been equally impressive in the manner of his Derby win, though the merit of his performance was probably not quite as high as the one at The Curragh. At Epsom he was never far from the hectic pace set by Mystiko and, having been sent to the front more than two furlongs out, he forged clear to win by five lengths.

The Derby added three new names to its distinguished roll of honour – owner Fahd Salman, trainer Paul Cole and jockey Alan Munro. It was Munro's first public appearance on the colt, following his appointment as Salman's retained rider. The

Alan Munro salutes a famous victory on Generous in the Irish Derby.

CAREER RECORD

Group race wins

1990 Three Chimneys Dewhurst Stakes

1991 Ever Ready Derby Stakes, Budweiser Irish Derby, King George VI and Queen Elizabeth Diamond Stakes

displacement of Richard Quinn seemed unfortunate, but while Quinn did his cause no harm by maintaining a diplomatic silence and riding winners, Munro advanced his by doing everything right on Generous.

Munro won the Derby, the Irish Derby and then the King George VI and Queen Elizabeth Diamond Stakes, where Generous passed his first test against older horses with a spectacular seven-length success. It was the fault of neither Munro nor Generous that the chestnut colt with the flaxen mane and tail – reminiscent of Grundy – never won again, and left the scene after the Arc.

It's a sponsor's delight as Generous, winner of the Derby at Epsom, completes a double in the Irish equivalent. His big rival Suave Dancer is beaten three lengths.

Persian War

Born 1963. By Persian Gulf out of Warning, by Chanteur.
Owned: Jakie Astor; Donald Leyland-Naylor; Henry Alper.
Trained: Dick Hern; Tom Masson; Brian Swift; Colin Davies;
Arthur Pitt; Dennis Rayson; Jack Gibson.

Persian War proves himself in a class of his own, winning his third Champion Hurdle in 1970. Major Rose (left), who finished second, is in fifth place at the last flight.

Trainers will say that the best owners are those who leave them alone to get on with the job. In that case, Henry Alper was one of the worst, for he took more than a close interest in his pride and joy, Persian War – his first horse, whom he bought after seeing him win on television.

Alper fell out with his first two trainers, Brian Swift and Colin Davies, despite their having won 14 races with Persian War, including three Champion Hurdles and the Triumph Hurdle, Schweppes Gold Trophy and Welsh Champion Hurdle. In all, Persian War had six trainers, counting an abortive spell with Pierre Sanoner in France, in the time he carried Alper's claret-and-blue 'West Ham' colours.

There were other upsets. Persian War badly injured his mouth in the only race he lost – apart from his highly promising debut, when he came third – as a juvenile hurdler. He fractured a femur in a fall in October 1968, the following year was jarred up by racing on firm ground on one of his sporadic returns to the Flat, and he later suffered from

a variety of wind ailments. It said much for his boundless courage that he overcame the setbacks to become one of the best horses ever to race over hurdles in Britain and Ireland.

Classically bred by Jakie Astor, he won two small staying races on the Flat for Dick Hern as a three-year-old and was sold for 3,600 guineas to Tom Masson, who trained him to win three hurdles races in the colours of Donald Leyland-Naylor. Then, enter Henry Alper and his chequebook.

Having won his first three races for his new connections and taken a knock at Kempton, Persian War won the four-year-old crown, the Triumph Hurdle, at Cheltenham. He had been entered for the Champion Hurdle but the temptation was resisted. It was a wise decision, for although Persian War's relentless gallop enabled him to shrug off the occasional lapse in his jumping, he would not have had the experience to cope with the best older horses in 1967. By the following year he had acquired, as well as a new trainer, the combination of speed, stamina and agility that was needed to begin a run of three Champion Hurdle victories that enabled him to emulate Hatton's Grace and Sir Ken.

In 1968 Persian War beat the favourite Chorus by four lengths; in 1969, starting favourite, he beat Drumikill by the same margin; and in 1970, again favourite, he had a harder fight, beating Major Rose by a length and a half. In 1971 he came back to try for an unprecedented fourth title, under the care of Arthur Pitt, and did marvellously well to finish four lengths second to Bula, with Major Rose third.

The nature of jump racing at this time meant that top-class horses appeared several times in high-value handicaps, and Persian War was no exception. He put up one of his finest performances when winning the Schweppes Gold Trophy in 1968, when under 11st 13lb he carried 5lb more than Major Rose and beat him by half a length in a 33-runner field. That, and his wins in the 1969 Welsh Champion Hurdle, where he beat Sempervivum by an easy two lengths conceding 6lb, and the 1970 Sweeps Hurdle, where he gave away weight to all his rivals and won by eight lengths, were as good as any of his efforts outside the Champion Hurdle.

Between leaving Tom Masson and joining Dennis Rayson, Persian War was ridden by Jimmy Uttley, a specialist hurdles jockey who had a remarkable wins-to-rides ratio. Martin Blackshaw was then given the ride, but there was a certain poignancy about Uttley's recall at Stratford on the last day of the 1971–72 season. Though he had not won in Britain for 18 months and was clearly on the decline, Persian War had everything in his favour and won. It was his last success before he was retired the following January.

Jimmy Uttley and Persian War take the final hurdle at Cheltenham in 1968 ahead of the favourite, Chorus.

CAREER RECORD

Major race wins

1966/67 Challow Hurdle, Victor Ludorum Hurdle, Daily Express Triumph Hurdle

1967/68 Schweppes Gold Trophy Hurdle, Champion Hurdle

1968/69 Champion Hurdle, Welsh Champion Hurdle

1969/70 Champion Hurdle

1970/71 Sweeps Hurdle

Night Nurse

Born 1971. By Falcon out of Florence Nightingale, by Above Suspicion. Owned: Charles Rudkin; Reg Spencer. Trained: Peter Easterby.

A study in styles as Paddy Broderick and Night Nurse fly over a hurdle at Newbury.

Northern Flat-race trainers have had an increasingly thin time against their southern colleagues over the last 25 years. But give them a big National Hunt race and they can invariably show the racing world a thing or two. That was the case with Peter Easterby in the 1970s, when his stable near Malton, Yorkshire, housed three of the leading jumpers in training – Night Nurse, Sea Pigeon and Alverton.

By virtue of winning two Champion Hurdles, finishing third in another and running second in the Cheltenham Gold Cup, Night Nurse can be considered the best of this bunch, though when he set out on his

Three in a line at the last flight in the 1977 Champion Hurdle, and Night Nurse (right) is too good for Monksfield (left) and Dramatist.

racing career, having been picked up as a yearling for 1,300 guineas, he looked nothing out of the ordinary.

It is not uncommon for some Flat-racers to improve out of all recognition when faced with eight flights of hurdles, and having gone through his first dozen races on the level with a single success for owner Charles Rudkin, Night Nurse was an instant hit over hurdles in the colours of Reg Spencer.

He won five times as a juvenile hurdler, showing that firmish going suited him well, and flopped only in the Triumph Hurdle, when racing was later abandoned because heavy rain had made the ground unsafe. He even translated his improvement to Flat racing and won twice in 1975 before embarking on a sequence of 18 hurdle races which produced 13 wins, four seconds and a third, beginning with ten victories in succession.

The unbeaten sequence took in an unusually dry winter, which resulted in largely firmish going, and Night Nurse surged to the top of the tree, improving markedly in ability and physical appearance. Attacking from the front for his regular partner Paddy Broderick, he won – among others – the Fighting Fifth Hurdle and Irish Sweeps Hurdle, when the weights were in his favour, and beat a Champion Hurdle field which included two previous winners in Comedy of Errors and Lanzarote, when conditions were the same for everyone.

The following year, 1977, brought evidence of Night Nurse's versatility, and he retained his hurdling crown in the mud, before going on to dead-heat with Monksfield at Liverpool over five furlongs farther than the Champion Hurdle. Both principals had very hard races at Liverpool, Night Nurse especially so since he had to recover from a bad mistake at the third-last flight, but he ran again ten days later and won the Welsh Champion Hurdle. No wonder he was voted National Hunt Horse of the Year for the second time.

This was Night Nurse's peak as a hurdler; thereafter Monksfield became his master, while Night Nurse had his attention turned to fences. With Broderick obliged to retire because of injuries received in a fall from Night Nurse at Kempton in December 1977, he was ridden by a number of jockeys

Hurdles or fences, they came alike to Night Nurse.

during the rest of his career. None was especially tender on him but he continued to give his all in dashing style.

His first season produced seven wins, including a victory over Dramatist at Liverpool that was almost as exciting as the battle with Monksfield and came only a fortnight after he had been asked to tackle the over-ambitious task for a novice of running in the Cheltenham Gold Cup. His second season was cut short by a leg injury, but he returned as good as new and beat all but his stablemate Little Owl in the 1981 Cheltenham Gold Cup. He returned for a crack at the title the following season, having shown himself to be still at his peak, but on the day, despite starting favourite, he was nowhere near being the Night Nurse of old. More than that, the familiar enthusiasm had gone. Though he soldiered on for four races, including one win, there was relief all round when it was announced, on the day of his twelfth birthday, that he had been retired.

CAREER RECORD

Major race wins

1975/76 Free Handicap Hurdle, Fighting Fifth Hurdle, Sweeps Hurdle, Champion Hurdle, Scottish Champion Hurdle, Welsh Champion Hurdle

1976/77 Marlow Ropes John Skeaping Hurdle, Champion Hurdle, Templegate Hurdle, Welsh Champion Hurdle

1977/78 William Hill Yorkshire Hurdle

1978/79 Bobby Renton Memorial Novices' Chase, Killiney Novices' Chase, Sean Graham Trophy Chase, London and Northern Group Future Champions Novices' Chase

1979/80 Buchanan Whisky Gold Cup Chase

1981/82 Bradstone Mandarin Handicap Chase

Burrough Hill Lad

Born 1976. By Richboy out of Green Monkey, by Court Martial. Owned: Stan Riley. Trained: Jimmy Harris; Harry Wharton; Jenny Pitman.

If only Burrough Hill Lad had been blessed with physical soundness to match his boundless enthusiasm and peerless talent ... He would not necessarily have improved in terms of ability, but he would have been in a better position to achieve the rewards he deserved. He might, for instance, have become the first horse since 1971 to win more than one Cheltenham Gold Cup; instead he was a late absentee from the race for two years in succession because of injury.

As it was, Burrough Hill Lad proved a smashing chaser, once his hurdling career had been put aside and once a consistency of trainer had been achieved. Bred by his owner, he was originally with three trainers in as many seasons, the first two of whom each won twice with him before he was sent home for the summer. Each time he failed to make it back to the same base, until, it seemed, owner Riley met his match in the redoubtable Jenny Pitman.

Mrs Pitman began the process of turning Burrough Hill Lad into a steeplechaser in the first week of 1982, and after a shaky start

Burrough Hill Lad (right) overcomes all the obstacles, including a tight track, which did not suit him, and Combs Ditch, who is alongside at the last fence, to win the King George VI Chase.

Two champions together, Burrough Hill Lad and John Francome.

she was rewarded with a win at Liverpool that promised much for the future. Progress was interrupted by precautionary withdrawal from training in November 1982, but he burst to the top the following season.

He won all his five races over fences in 1983–84, beginning with the Welsh National, where he carried 3lb overweight at 10st 6lb for John Francome's services; and ending with the Cheltenham Gold Cup, where his jockey Phil Tuck kept him to the inside up the straight and beat the drifting Brown Chamberlin (ridden by Francome) by three lengths.

Burrough Hill Lad had improved by a stone and a half throughout the season, but there was better to come, including five more wins in a row. The sequence started with an outstanding effort under 12st in the Hennessy Cognac Gold Cup at Newbury and ended with a walkover at Sandown which sent his first-prize earnings to a record level for Britain and Ireland. In between came one of his best runs, to beat Combs Ditch by a short head in the King George VI Chase at Kempton, a course which did not entirely suit him but where raw courage enabled him to prevail.

In the event, that King George VI Chase was to be his last major level-weights success, through force of circumstance rather than consistent loss of form, though he did run unaccountably badly in the 1985 King George and had an owner-enforced change of jockey as a result. He still showed himself to be, on balance, the best staying chaser in the country, running a marvellous race under 12st 7lb to finish third in the SGB Handicap Chase and winning Sandown's Gainsborough Handicap Chase, for the third time, under 12st.

As in 1985 he missed the Cheltenham Gold Cup because of injury, and leg trouble kept him off the course for all the next season. He returned to the track at Wincanton in February 1988, and though last of three runners, showed enough promise to suggest he was not ready to be pensioned off. Three weeks later he finished lame after a racecourse exercise spin and both owner and trainer decided that retirement was the best course of action. His relentless gallop had finally been brought to an end.

CAREER RECORD

Major race wins

1981/82 Siematic Kitchens Novices' Chase

1982/83 Sean Graham Chase

1983/84 Coral Welsh National Handicap Chase, Anthony Mildmay Peter Cazalet Memorial Handicap Chase, Gainsborough Handicap Chase, Tote Cheltenham Gold Cup Chase

1984/85 Hennessy Cognac Gold Cup Handicap Chase, Charlie Hall Memorial Wetherby Pattern Chase, King George VI Chase, Gainsborough Handicap Chase (walkover)

1985/86 Rehearsal Chase, Gainsborough Handicap Chase

Desert Orchid

Born 1979. By Grey Mirage out of Flower Child, by Brother. Owned: Richard Burridge and partners. Trained: David Elsworth.

Desert Orchid leads the field on his way to winning the 1989 Cheltenham Gold Cup. It wasn't his best performance, but it was easily his most popular.

Arkle, Red Rum, Desert Orchid: they have been the most popular horses of the last 25 years – all steeplechasers, incidentally – but which one was *the* most popular? The answer has to be Desert Orchid, at least when he was racing.

Arkle was the best; Red Rum enjoyed unprecedented public support during his retirement; but Desert Orchid was the one that racecourses could rely on to bring in the extra crowds.

Desert Orchid enjoys two advantages over Arkle and Red Rum: he is a grey, going on snowy-white, and therefore instantly recognisable; and he came along at a time when media interest, whether through television, radio or newspapers and magazines, was at its most consuming.

He had other qualities going for him – not least his style of running, which meant he was usually racing along at the head of the field, attacking his fences with great gusto, as well as giving a hint of impending

Desert Orchid on the racecourse and at home. Richard Dunwoody guides him to his second victory in the King George VI Rank Chase (above), and (right) pride in his appearance suffers after a roll in the mud.

disaster. He did fall on his very first appearance, in a hurdle race at Kempton in January 1983, and was always inclined to make a mistake or two in his races. With supreme irony he fell on his last appearance, also at Kempton, on Boxing Day 1991; but these were exceptions which proved the general rule that he usually got himself out of trouble.

He was no slouch over hurdles, moving to the top of the tree as a novice to such good purpose that he ran in the Champion Hurdle in his second season, having started the term without a win to his name. He stayed over hurdles for another season, but it was when he went steeplechasing in November 1985 that he really began to blossom.

After four straight wins he ran well against the best novices, but not well enough to beat them. The following season, though, he took their measure and so began a record of four wins and a second in the King George VI Chase at Kempton.

In 1986, he made all the running and won by 15 lengths from Bolands Cross. In 1988, he started odds on and won smoothly by four lengths from Kildimo. In 1989, he was again odds on and won without a serious challenge by eight lengths from Barnbrook Again. And in 1990 he galloped home 12 lengths ahead of Toby Tobias. Only 1987 spoiled the sequence, when he was beaten 15 lengths by Nupsala and would not have finished second but for a last-fence fall by Forgive 'N Forget.

Curiously, Colin Brown did not win a King George on Desert Orchid, though he rode him 44 times for 17 wins. Simon Sherwood (nine wins out of ten rides) and Richard Dunwoody (seven out of 15) shared the King George equally. Richard Linley (one out of one) and Graham Bradley (unplaced in one) were the only other jockeys to ride Desert Orchid over jumps, while Brian Rouse rode him in his single, unplaced outing on the Flat as a six-year-old.

Desert Orchid's King George victories added up to a record, as did his prize-money earnings – £652,802 – for a jumper trained in Britain and Ireland, and his four Horse of the Year awards.

Once considered no more than a two-miler, he revealed more stamina with age and put up several fine performances outside the King George VI Chase, notably

Work is over for the day, and while regular rider Rodney Boult takes the easy way home, trainer David Elsworth offers the reward of a mint.

in the 1987 Whitbread Gold Cup, where he made almost all the running and beat off the determined challenge of Kildimo up the final hill at Sandown; and the 1990 Irish Grand National, where he carried 26lb more than any other runner and survived an almighty blunder at the last fence. His best effort, according to the official handicapper, was in the 1990 Racing Post Chase at Kempton, where he carried 12st 3lb, made much of the running, and jumped brilliantly to win by eight lengths from Delius, with the same distance from Delius to the subsequent Grand National winner Seagram.

These were all smashing efforts, worthy of a champion and guaranteed to take him and his closest connections – owner Richard Burridge, trainer David Elsworth and lass Janice Coyle – on to the main non-sporting pages of the newspapers. But they were nothing compared to the acclaim he received for winning the Cheltenham Gold Cup in 1989. It was his sixth consecutive outing at the Cheltenham Festival, but in a variety of races – from the Champion Hurdle to the Champion Chase – he had always failed, sometimes honourably, sometimes less so. This time it was different, and even those in the 50,000 crowd who had not backed him gave the impression they wanted him to win as he tackled and headed Yahoo on the gruelling, uphill run-in. Desert Orchid did it by a length and a half. That had to be his finest hour.

CAREER RECORD

Major race wins

1983/84 Kingwell Pattern Hurdle

1984/85 Oteley Hurdle

1985/86 Henry VIII Novices' Chase, Killiney Novices' Chase

1986/87 King George VI Rank Chase

1987/88 Terry Biddlecombe Trophy Chase, Rank Boxing Day Trial Chase, Chevas Regal Cup Chase, Whitbread Gold Cup Handicap Chase

1988/89 Terry Biddlecombe Trophy Chase, Tingle Creek Handicap Chase, King George VI Rank Chase, Victor Chandler Handicap Chase, Racecall Gainsborough Handicap Chase, Tote Cheltenham Gold Cup Chase

1989/90 King George VI Rank Chase, Racing Post Handicap Chase, Jameson Irish Grand National Handicap Chase

1990/91 King George VI Rank Chase, Agfa Diamond Handicap Chase

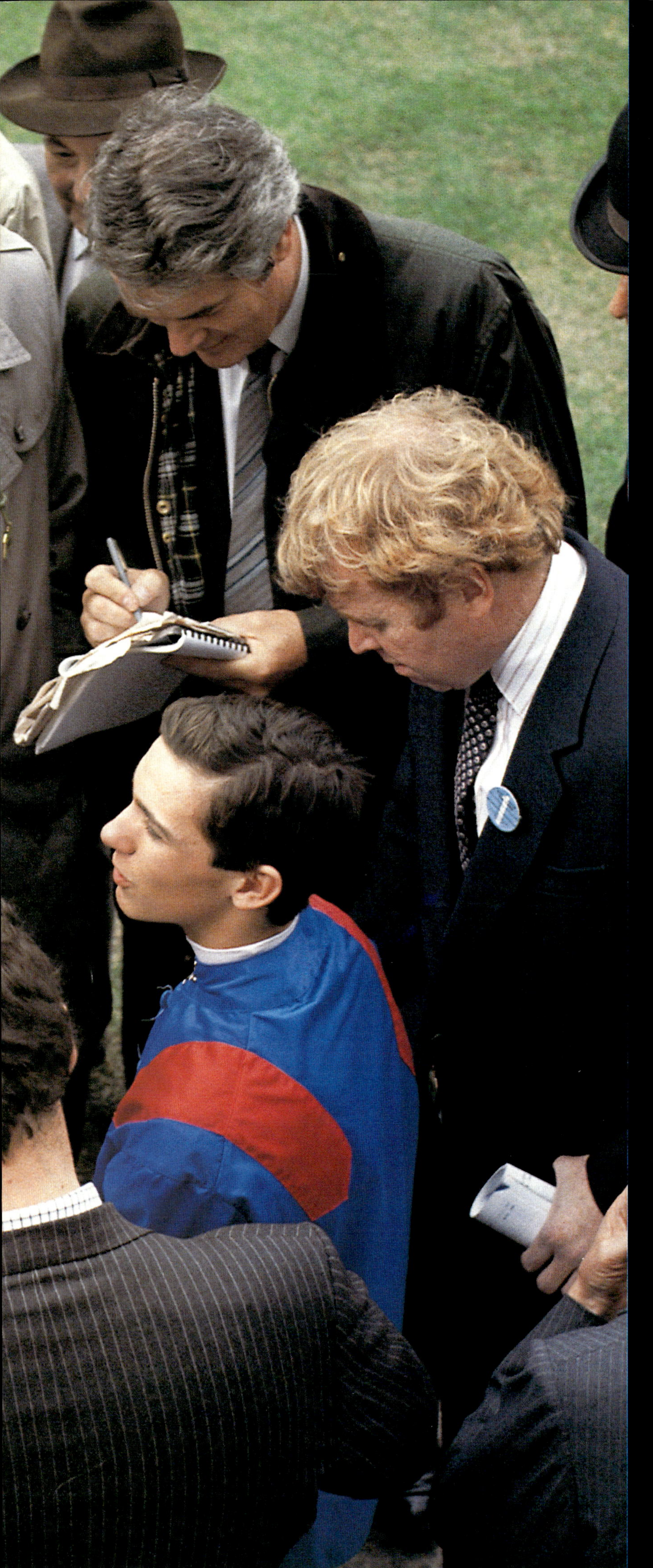

Great Jockeys

Horses generally make jockeys, but just occasionally a jockey will make a horse. That's the difference between an ordinary rider and one who is on his way to becoming a Great Jockey.

Making the fewest mistakes is another attribute which marks out the best from the better-than-average. And winning a race when under any other circumstances the horse should have been beaten is the most compelling evidence of star quality.

Yet who is to say that Lester Piggott, with nine Derby winners to his credit, is a better jockey than Sir Gordon Richards, who won the race only once? And who can argue with conviction whether Yves Saint-Martin, the best in France since the War, is a better jockey than Bill Shoemaker, who has ridden more winners than any other rider in the world?

Once the debate moves into the highest league, it becomes a matter of opinion.

No one should doubt that the ten Great Jockeys detailed here are worthy of being compared with the best. Each has his own qualities: two are based in the United States, one came from there to join three others on the Flat in Britain, Saint-Martin has been mentioned, and three made their name over jumps.

There will be others who deserve a vote, which illustrates how rich is today's stock of riders. But is it any more bountiful than in the days of Richards, Wragg and Smirke, or Smith, Breasley and Hutchinson? That's a matter of opinion.

Perhaps more to the point, where are the names that may topple some of the Top Ten here?

WILLIE CARSON

Six years was a long time to get established, but Willie Carson has stayed the course better, and more successfully, than most.

Head down, body crouched, arms pumping, perfectly balanced: the style belongs unmistakably to Willie Carson. Few can match his level of consistency in recent years and his energy belies the fact that he reaches his fiftieth birthday in November 1992

Perhaps a slow start has helped Carson towards a sustained finish; it certainly enabled him to keep his feet on the ground when success did arrive.

The Queen Mother makes a point as Willie Carson takes the Ritz Club Trophy as leading jockey at Royal Ascot in 1983.

Born in Stirling, the son of a warehouseman and a waitress, he began in racing with Gerald Armstrong at Middleham in Yorkshire and his name first appeared on a race card in May 1959. Three years and two months later he rode his first winner, and after another three years he had gathered enough winners to lose his apprentice riding allowance. He could hardly be termed an overnight success.

Moving to Newmarket in 1962 to join Armstrong's brother Sam gave Carson's career its impetus, and teaming up with Bernard van Cutsem two years later provided its stability. He went from riding handicappers to being associated with class horses and rode his first Classic winner in the 1972 2,000 Guineas on High Top. That year, he was champion jockey for the first of five times, following up his success in 1973, 1978, 1980 and 1983.

That he has not been champion jockey since is no reflection on his own standards, for he has continued a remarkable run of riding at least one hundred winners in 20 of the last 21 years. He recovered from a serious accident in 1981 and, helped by his natural light weight, he has provided the most telling answer to those who suggested his career might be on the wane.

He had more rides than any other jockey in 1991, and his winning totals in the last four seasons are proof positive that he is riding with the skill of a top-class artist and the energy of a man half his age. He even registered his highest score, 187, in 1990, highlighted by six winners on one momentous day at Newcastle, and was foiled of the championship only because Pat Eddery became the first for 38 years to clock more than two hundred winners.

Carson's loyalty is well established. Following van Cutsem's untimely death in 1975, he has had only three retainers – he was with Clive Brittain for a single year, with Dick Hern for 12 years, and since 1990 has been with Hern's chief patron, Hamdan Al-Maktoum. His support during Hern's accident and later illness earned him more than token respect.

All but a handful of Carson's greatest triumphs, including 16 British Classic successes, have been shared with Hern; they range from three Derby wins – Troy, Henbit and his own favourite, Nashwan – to the Queen's Silver Jubilee year Classic triumphs with Dunfermline and the poignant St Leger success of Minster Son, whom Carson bred and rode to win while Hern was temporarily out of action.

With more than 3,200 career wins, Carson is third behind Sir Gordon Richards and Lester Piggott in the all-time list of winning British jockeys, having overtaken Doug Smith, whom he succeeded at van Cutsem's stable, in 1990. Only Pat Eddery stands close enough to knock him off this particular perch; whether Carson intends giving him any time to try unopposed remains to be seen.

Further reward for Royal jockey Willie Carson, who was appointed OBE in the 1983 New Year's Honours list.

Dunfermline crowns the Queen's Silver Jubilee year by winning the St Leger, where the hot favourite Alleged has to give best.

Steve Cauthen

From Kentucky to Kempton Park, Steve Cauthen made the journey look easy, and is the only champion jockey on both sides of the Atlantic.

A top-class sportsman will prove himself anywhere and under any conditions, so it was not surprising that Steve Cauthen showed himself more than a match for the weather on a wet, filthy day at Salisbury on 7 April 1979, when he coaxed Marquee Universal home first past the post.

It was Cauthen's first ride in Britain, a much publicized event featuring the Kentucky Kid, the Six Million Dollar Man, who had arrived from his native United States a month before his twentieth birthday, seemingly after his astonishing riding career had taken a turn for the worse.

Cauthen was just 16 when he rode his first winner in 1976; the following year he rode 487 winners from 2,075 rides to earn $6 million, and in 1978 he won the US Triple Crown on Affirmed, whose battles with Alydar became legend. Then followed a losing run of more than one hundred rides and, at the invitation of Robert Sangster and Barry Hills, Cauthen decided to try Britain. The move could not have worked out better.

He adapted readily to the British way of life and racing, and with his accent becoming less unfamiliar there are times when he seems more British than the British. His quiet, unassuming but authoritative manner, allied to an unflurried but forceful ability to produce the best from the best horses, has brought him a big following among racegoers.

He won the 2,000 Guineas on Tap on Wood in his first year and gradually improved his scores so that in 1984, with 130 winners, he became the first American since

The style soon became familiar but this was the first time British racegoers had seen Steve Cauthen in action. On his Salisbury debut he sends Marquee Universal past Twickenham.

1908 to be champion jockey in Britain, and the first rider ever to top the table on both sides of the Atlantic. In 1985 he succeeded Lester Piggott as stable jockey for Henry Cecil, and was champion again that year and in 1987. He is the only jockey to have broken the championship domination of Pat Eddery.

The first year of the Cauthen–Cecil partnership coincided with the emergence of the colt Slip Anchor and the filly Oh So Sharp, and with them he won four of the five Classics. Slip Anchor enabled Cauthen to become the first jockey to win the Kentucky Derby and Epsom Derby (he has since added another with Reference Point, and equivalents in Ireland and France with Old Vic), while Oh So Sharp's wins in the 1,000 Guineas, Oaks and St Leger meant he was the first to win a Triple Crown (of sorts ...) in the States and Britain. Reference Point gave him a second Derby success, as well as wins in the King George VI and Queen Elizabeth Diamond Stakes and St Leger, in 1987; he won the Oaks the following year on Diminuendo and the St Leger in 1989 on Michelozzo.

All his working life Cauthen has had to wage war against the scales – he is naturally about a stone above his minimum riding weight of 8st 7lb – and at one period in the late 1980s it seemed he was losing the battle. Inevitably, he will give up the fight one day, almost certainly well before the age at which most of his serious rivals retire, and it is likely that he will return to his native America. British racing will be the poorer for his eventual departure.

PAT EDDERY

Champion apprentice, then champion jockey. Only Pat Eddery has ridden more than two hundred winners in a British Flat season in the last 40 years.

If the cap fits: that's a winning smile from Pat Eddery after his 1991 St Leger victory on Toulon.

Every sport has a professionals' professional, and Pat Eddery is Flat racing's. Less outwardly chirpy than Willie Carson and less obviously approachable than Steve Cauthen, his biggest rivals for supremacy over the last ten years, he has made his mark where it matters most, on the racecourse.

Eddery typifies the modern top-class jockey: employed directly by a wealthy owner (Khalid Abdullah), rather than retained by one or more trainers; riding six days a week from March to November and at two meetings on many days in summer; flying to the races from his stud-farm home in Buckinghamshire and as likely to be seen in France as he is in England, with at least one working trip to the United States each year; and well rewarded.

He turned 40 this year and has been at the top for half that time. Apprenticed to Seamus McGrath in his native Ireland at the age of 14, he came to England a year later to join the noted tutor Frenchie Nicholson and though a year went by between his first ride and his first win in this country, he was champion apprentice in 1971. Three years later he was champion jockey and won his first Classic, on Polygamy in the Oaks.

It sounds easy, and Eddery has made it look that way, but natural ability is not everything. Dedication, determination and a passion for riding have kept him at the height of his profession, logging a record

There's concentration written on their faces as Pat Eddery (right) and Steve Cauthen race neck and neck into the last week of the 1987 jockeys' championship. Cauthen got there by 197 winners to 195, but Eddery has won the last four titles.

which includes winning the Prix de l'Arc de Triomphe four times (on Detroit, Rainbow Quest, Dancing Brave and Trempolino), the Derby three times (Grundy, Golden Fleece and Quest For Fame) and other British Classics six times.

No British-based jockey has a better recent record in the hothouse atmosphere of America's biggest races, where Eddery has won the Arlington Million (on Tolomeo), and two Breeders' Cup races – the Turf on Pebbles and the Sprint on Sheikh Albadou. All distances, all surfaces and all countries seem to come alike to him.

Continuity has been a key in Eddery's career, and he has had only four major associations since he left Dublin for Britain in 1967. Leaving Nicholson in 1973, he rode for Peter Walwyn for seven years and succeeded Lester Piggott as stable jockey to Vincent O'Brien until 1987, since when he has been wearing the Abdullah colours.

Each stage has been marked by a series of highlights outside his collection of big-race successes. With Walwyn he was champion jockey four times; with O'Brien he was champion once in Ireland, though based in Britain; and with Abdullah he has won the title each season since 1988.

Additionally, in 1990 he became the first jockey since Gordon Richards in 1952 to ride more than two hundred winners in a season. In July 1991 he rode his three-thousandth winner in Britain, and some time in 1992 he should overtake Doug Smith and move into fourth place in the all-time list, with Willie Carson – ten years senior to Eddery – the next target.

Eddery was quicker than the four ahead of him to reach three thousand winners, taking a little over 22 years, compared with 24 by Sir Gordon Richards, 27 by Lester Piggott, 28 by Carson and 33 by Smith. Only Carson has shared Eddery's advantages of more racing and better and faster communications, but both have had to contend with the increased competition of recent years. With time on his side and his enthusiasm apparently undiminished, Eddery seems poised for even greater rewards.

Lester Piggott

It looked like the end of a great sporting career when Lester Piggott went to prison. But it was just the start of another amazing chapter.

The crowds willed on Lester Piggott to win his comeback race at Leicester on Lupescu. But Gary Carter and Sumonda (far side) spoilt the party.

When Lester Piggott walked out to ride Lupescu in the 2.15 race at Leicester on 15 October 1990, a crowd of around three thousand – twice as many as the track would normally attract on an autumn Monday afternoon – buzzed with anticipation. When he returned a few minutes later, beaten a short head by a jockey less than half his age, the eyes of the racing world and beyond were still on him. The second coming of Piggott had begun, and people still wondered if they should dare to believe what they were seeing.

Almost exactly five years previously, Piggott, a month short of his fiftieth birthday, had ridden in England for what was thought to be the last time. Since then he had taken up training, with mixed results, and had spent a year in prison for tax evasion. Refused a trainer's licence while he was serving his final period of parole, he popped up in the saddle in Peru of all places in December 1989. The following July he rode in two veterans' invitation races in Ireland, but still no one but his closest confidante could have imagined the name L Piggott would be back on the official race cards – at least not until the Jockey Club announced out of the blue on 11 October 1990 that Piggott had been passed 'medically fit in all respects to hold a jockey's licence'.

The day after his return Piggott rode a

It was as if Lester Piggott had never been away, and within a fortnight of his return (right) he was watching with relish a replay of his winning ride on Royal Academy in the Breeders' Cup Mile.

winner at Chepstow, appropriately trained by his wife Susan, and it was almost as if he had never been away. The hair was greyer but the inimitable, high-in-the-stirrups style was still there. And within no time Piggott was definitely back, incredibly winning a race on Breeders' Cup day at New York's Belmont Park on Royal Academy for his old guvnor Vincent O'Brien. It was only 12 days into his return and the Americans couldn't believe it. Nor could some of the Brits in the crowd, let alone those watching at home on television. It was Piggott at his best, rousting Royal Academy for a surge up the straight right to the front in the last few strides.

France, Northern Ireland, Italy, Spain, all-weather at Southwell, India, Hong Kong: they all saw Piggott in action before he returned to start a new turf season in 1991. When he stood up at the inaugural Jockeys Association Awards dinner at the end of March to receive a Sports Person of the Year nomination from his fellow professionals, the prolonged standing ovation said it all.

Never one to use two words when one will suffice, Piggott remains revered by his weighing-room colleagues – even those who have had to stand aside while he stepped into their shoes for a big-race ride – and is a hero to the racegoing public, who remember his 4,349 winners between 1948 and 1985; his 11 jockeys' championships; and his Classic wins, among them nine Derby victories; seven King George VI and Queen Elizabeth Stakes triumphs; and 25 centuries in a season, all records.

In the last 25 years they remember his fabulous Anglo-Irish partnership with O'Brien; his brilliance on such as Sir Ivor, Nijinsky, Roberto, The Minstrel; his return to an English base for Henry Cecil in 1981 and two subsequent jockeys' titles. They remember when he was sentenced to three years' imprisonment.

Once back on the outside in October 1987, Piggott seemed like a lost soul. Riding racehorses had been his life from the time he was apprenticed to his father Keith at the age of 12; training had never consumed him in the same way. Maybe it was inevitable that he would resume race-riding, even at an age when most men are thinking of nothing more strenuous than a leisurely round of golf. It was the best move he could have made – for himself, for those who remember him at his peak, and for a new generation who can appreciate what all the fuss was about. The proof came when he won his thirtieth Classic on Rodrigo de Triano in the 2,000 Guineas in May 1992.

Laffit Pincay

Laffit Pincay started in racing working for nothing. Nearly 7,800 winners later, he is in the top two jockeys for races won and prize-money earned.

Bayakoa's owners paid $200,000 to enter her for the Breeders' Cup Distaff in 1989. Laffit Pincay makes sure it was worthwhile.

When American owner-breeder Fred Hooper was on the look-out for a new jockey, he used to turn to Panama. There he found Braulio Baeza, Jorge Velasquez and the top of the bill, Laffit Pincay.

Born in December 1946, the son of a jockey, Pincay was so keen to get into racing that he began working as a groom in Panama City at the age of 15 for no reward other than the experience. He rode his first winner in 1964 and two years later was on his way to the States, where he now stands second only to Bill Shoemaker as the world's winningmost jockey and is engaged in a close and prolonged tussle with Angel

Pound for pound Laffit Pincay continues to punch his weight at the top of the American jockeys' lists.

Cordero for achieving the most earnings by a single rider. Pincay's tally stands at around $165 million!

Phenomenally high prize-money and year-round racing with nine or ten races at each meeting give American jockeys the chance to build up records which the rest of the racing world can only dream about. But they still need achieving, and Pincay's strength and will to win first propelled him to the top and since have enabled him to stay there.

Though he rode his first Stateside winner, in July 1966, at Chicago's Arlington Park, California has been his long-time base; having surpassed Shoemaker's record earnings in 1985, he took another shot off the great American early in 1992 when he became the most successful jockey at Santa Anita with more than 2,250 winners. Pincay's career total is nearing 7,800, compared with Shoemaker's closing score of 8,833.

Pincay's success has to be judged in the light of his weight disadvantage. As well as having to seek professional advice to control unwanted poundage, he had to face up to the lighter American scale from a mark of around 8st 5lb, compared with Shoemaker's tidy 7st 0lb.

The difference means Pincay's choice of rides has been more limited ... but only by comparison with Shoemaker. Seven times US champion jockey for earnings, and once for races won, Pincay has won America's top racing honour, the Eclipse Award, five times, more than any other jockey, and was elected to the Hall of Fame in 1975.

It is a measure of his standing, even as he reaches the veteran stage, that in eight years and 56 races of the hotly contested Breeders' Cup, he has had 47 rides. In this series alone his mounts, including six winners, have won more than $6 million.

Bayakoa, who twice won the Distaff, and Skywalker, who turned over two better-fancied rivals in the Classic, are the best of his Breeders' Cup winners. They belong in a personal Hall of Fame which also includes Affirmed, on whom he took over from Steve Cauthen as a four-year-old; the tough turf champion John Henry; and three straight Belmont Stakes winners in Conquistador Cielo, Caveat and Swale, who also won the Kentucky Derby.

Bill Shoemaker

Ninety-five pounds of pure genius in the saddle. Bill Shoemaker was quick off the mark and steadily made his way to a world record for winners.

Twenty-five years ago, Bill Shoemaker was already the world's most outstanding active jockey; now he stands as a racing legend, though sadly he is seriously paralysed as the result of a road accident in April 1991.

Born in Texas in 1931, Shoemaker found fame in California, where he left school to work on a training farm before becoming an exercise rider at the local tracks. He rode his first winner in April 1949 and by the end of that year had won 219 races. That's how quickly the tiny Texan – 4ft 11ins and weighing 95lb – took America by storm. By 1966 he had amassed five numerical championships in North America and ten for money earned, both records. He had ridden 485 winners in one season, then a world record, and he had been elected to the Hall of Fame in 1958. He had won the Kentucky Derby on Swaps (1955), Tomy Lee (1959) and Lucky Debonair (1965).

Over the years covered by this volume Shoemaker was never champion jockey, but his standing continued to soar. In September 1970 he rode his 6,033rd winner, to overtake Johnny Longden as the most successful jockey in international racing history, and when he retired in February 1990 – having ridden in six decades – his score stood at 8,833.

Despite Shoemaker's relentless progress away from Longden's total, quality rather than quantity was the feature of his latter career. Big races became his speciality, and it was no surprise that he was the man who won the first million-dollar race in America, the Arlington Million, on John Henry in

1981, or that he became the oldest jockey to win the Kentucky Derby and a Breeders' Cup race, both achieved on Ferdinand in 1986 and 1987.

Ferdinand was trained by Charlie Whittingham, with whom Shoemaker forged a most fruitful partnership, involving such other big winners as Ack Ack, Cougar, Exceller and Galaxy Libra. John Henry was an example of a connection that Shoemaker made on account of his being the best man for the best horse in the best races – others included Damascus, winner of the Preakness and Belmont Stakes; Spectacular Bid, unbeaten as a four-year-old in 1980; and the giant gelding Forego, three times Horse of the Year.

As Shoemaker grew older he began to broaden his international reputation, though his quiet yet forceful style was not seen in

Tipping the scales at 95 lb (above), Bill Shoemaker more than matched other jockeys for strength, and has outridden all of them for winners. His biggest successes include the world's first million-dollar race on John Henry (left).

Britain until 1978. He had been to Europe 13 years earlier, riding the Preakness Stakes winner Tom Rolfe to finish sixth behind Sea-Bird in the Prix de l'Arc de Triomphe, but it was not until Robert Sangster persuaded him to come to Epsom for the Derby that an English crowd saw him in action. The plan all but succeeded and after making all the running on Hawaiian Sound, Shoemaker was only touched off near the line by Shirley Heights. He became a more frequent visitor to Europe and rode his first winner here in a match against Lester Piggott in 1982. Two years later there was no more popular win at Royal Ascot than his success on Sikorsky in a handicap.

Yves Saint-Martin

The idol of the Paris tracks, Yves Saint-Martin took his riding talents around the racecourses of the world and won over the crowds with charm and style.

Surrounded by the signs of history, Yves Saint-Martin receives part of his reward for winning the 200th St Leger on Crow. The Levy Board chairman Lord Plummer hands over the commemorative jockey's cap.

French jockeys generally have had a poor reputation in Britain since the War, and few have seemed able to handle with any consistency the unfamiliar tracks and different racing rhythm. The most notable exception is Yves Saint-Martin, an artist, stylist and brilliant judge of pace who made himself as much at home at Ascot, Doncaster, Epsom and Newmarket as around his native courses in the Paris region.

It is ironic that Saint-Martin fell off on his first ride in public and finished last on his final two mounts, but between those two events – at Soissons, north-east of Paris, in 1958, and at Bay Meadows, in California, in January 1988 – he was always at or near the top of his profession in France and enjoyed enormous international respect.

Born in 1941, he was apprenticed to François Mathet shortly after his fourteenth birthday but two and a half years passed before he was allowed to ride in public. In 1960, at the age of 19, he was champion jockey for the first of a record 15 times, with

109 winners. He remained with Mathet, one of the old school of disciplinarians, until 1971, after which his two lasting retainers were for Daniel Wildenstein and the Aga Khan.

Saint-Martin's first Classic winner in Britain, the short-head Oaks heroine Monade in 1962, was not trained by Mathet but they won that year's King George VI and Queen Elizabeth Stakes with Match and returned to Epsom the following year to land the Derby with Relko.

Having added to his list of British Classic wins the 1,000 Guineas on Altesse Royale in 1971 for Noel Murless and 2,000 Guineas on Nonoalco in 1974 for François Boutin, Saint-Martin had his finest season in this country in 1976, when in the Wildenstein colours he won the 1,000 Guineas on Flying Water, the Oaks and King George VI and Queen Elizabeth Diamond Stakes on Pawneese and the St Leger on Crow. Here without doubt was a jockey for whom colts and fillies, milers and stayers, left- and right-handed tracks came alike.

In France he reigned supreme, winning the Prix de l'Arc de Triomphe for all three retainers – for Mathet on Sassafras in 1970, for Wildenstein on Allez France (1974) and Sagace (1984), and for the Aga Khan on Akiyda (1982). And he won the Prix du Jockey-Club (French Derby) a record nine times, the first on Reliance in 1965 and the last on Natroun in his retirement year.

He is on record as regarding the Arc victory of Sassafras over Lester Piggott and Nijinsky as his most satisfying, while the various exploits of Allez France, on whom he displayed such exquisite timing, gave him the most pleasure. But when asked about his greatest moment, he turns to the United States and nominates Lashkari's winning the first Breeders' Cup Turf race – beating the Wildenstein-owned All Along – in 1984.

From limited opportunities Saint-Martin enjoyed remarkable success in North America, where he first showed off his talent to win the Washington DC International in 1962 on Match. He won a second Breeders' Cup race, the Sprint, on Last Tycoon, and had the last big-race success of a career totalling more than 3,300 winners on Khariyda in the E P Taylor Stakes at Woodbine.

Despite a career studded with injury, Saint-Martin retired fit and healthy. He decided he simply had nothing left to prove. Though he once said he would take up training in the States when he finished riding, he has remained in France, where a number of business ventures and promotional work occupy his time outside keeping fit and watching the progress of his jockey son, Eric.

Weight never bothered Yves Saint-Martin as a jockey, though he appears to be looking apprehensively at the weighing-room display.

John Francome

Style was John Francome's hallmark as a jockey. It took him to a record number of winners over jumps, and from there to a career in the media.

Ask anyone to name the most stylish jockeys over jumps in the last 25 years and the name of John Francome will be top of the list. He was also one of the two most successful riders of the time, taking the record for most winners from Stan Mellor in 1984 and only surrendering it to the onslaught of Peter Scudamore.

Francome might have made a career as an international show jumper – he was a junior champion who rode for Britain – and the experience was not lost on him when he turned to jump racing. There was no one better at presenting a horse at a fence, or measuring a stride to the inch, and he won more than one race 'out in the country'. Gradually he added judgement of pace and strength in a finish to his armoury, and at his peak he could be described as the complete jump jockey.

Throughout his 16-year riding career

John Francome's strength as a jockey was perfect timing and Musso makes jumping the water at Newbury look easy.

Fred Winter's backing helped John Francome towards the record number of winners by a jump jockey.

Francome was associated with Fred Winter's Lambourn stable. The continuity was invaluable and Winter's personal loyalty immeasurable, especially in helping Francome through a sticky period when he fell foul of the Jockey Club over his association with bookmaker John Banks.

Francome rode a winner on his first ride in December 1970 and was to succeed Richard Pitman as Fred Winter's stable jockey in 1975. For him he won the Cheltenham Gold Cup in 1978 on Midnight Court, as well as such big races as the Hennessy Cognac Gold Cup and the Sun Alliance Chase on Brown Chamberlin, the Kennedy Construction Gold Cup on Observe, and Embassy Premier Chase finals on Floating Pound and The Dealer.

Yet, perhaps surprisingly, Francome's two most notable achievements, as well as one other equally famous victory, came for trainers other than Winter.

His winning ride on Sea Pigeon for Peter Easterby in the 1981 Champion Hurdle, where he was a late replacement for the injured Jonjo O'Neill, saw Francome at his best as he delayed using the gelding's speed until well after the last flight. And his handling of Burrough Hill Lad for Jenny Pitman took him to the top of the steeple-chasing tree with superb wins in the Welsh National, Hennessy Cognac Gold Cup and King George VI Chase. His earlier King George win on Wayward Lad for Michael Dickinson began this talented chaser's record-breaking run in the Boxing Day feature.

Champion jockey seven times – once sharing the title with Peter Scudamore when he deliberately gave up before the end of the season after he had matched the score of his injured rival – Francome rode over one hundred winners in each of his last five seasons and established his highest total of 131 in 1983-84. He announced his retirement after a fall from The Reject on 9 April 1985 and bowed out, aged 32, with 1,138 career wins from 5,072 mounts.

For a brief period he turned his hand to training, from a Lambourn yard he built himself, but having sold those premises to Barry Hills on his return from Manton, he was foiled in finding a suitable alternative and gave up altogether. He quickly made a name for himself in the media, first as a knowledgeable and entertaining presenter of racing on television and more recently as a more than capable writer and co-author.

Jonjo O'Neill

They don't come any braver than Jonjo O'Neill. Having won a famous victory on Dawn Run, he soon had a bigger fight on his hands to beat serious illness.

As the slim, smiling figure in top hat and morning suit strode into the winner's enclosure at Royal Ascot, the cheers would have done more credit to a Gold Cup than one of the junior two-year-old races at the meeting. Four years earlier, in 1986, the same smiling figure had ridden in to a tumultuous reception after winning the Cheltenham Gold Cup. Then the ovation was directed as much towards his partner, Dawn Run; now the applause and delight was unashamedly for the man himself, Jonjo O'Neill.

It was June 1990 and O'Neill had trained the winner of the Windsor Castle Stakes in Gypsy Fiddler. Nothing too extraordinary in that, but this was a public show of affection, and relief, for a man who endeared himself to racing fans in a way that few other jockeys have matched. Not only had he notched a record for winners in a jump season – 149 in 1977–78 – but he had also battled back from a succession of terrible injuries and, most serious of all, he had beaten cancer.

When O'Neill retired from riding in May 1986, with two jockeys' titles and 901 jumps winners to his name, those around him were pleased that physical anguish and the perpetual fear of broken bones were behind him. He was about to start training from his home near Penrith. Three months later the racing world was told he was suffering from cancer. O'Neill put on a brave face for the public, showing the same fortitude which had shone through his riding career.

Born in Fermoy, Co. Cork, in April 1952, O'Neill rode a few winners on the Flat, over hurdles and over fences before he arrived in England in February 1972 to join Gordon Richards' Penrith stable, where he stayed until turning freelance in 1977. That was the season he broke the record for most winners in a season by a British jump jockey, held by his great friend Ron Barry with 125.

Night Nurse is one of many top-class jumpers who showed their style with Jonjo O'Neill.

In the next eight years he experienced

some of the greatest heights: winning the Cheltenham Gold Cup in 1979 on Alverton and the Champion Hurdle the following year on Sea Pigeon, and completing a unique double in these races on the great mare Dawn Run in 1984 and 1986. He even won one of the season's hottest handicaps on the Flat, on Sea Pigeon. But he also saw the sadder side: missing Sea Pigeon's second Champion Hurdle victory because of a badly broken leg, and crashing as Alverton broke his neck in a fatal fall in the Grand National.

Only Desert Orchid's Cheltenham Gold Cup victory can match that of Dawn Run for public enthusiasm, and half the acclaim was for O'Neill, not the most stylish jockey who ever rode jumpers, but one who gave his mounts every assistance and a little bit more when it mattered. He was hard to beat in a finish, and the welcome at Royal Ascot showed what the public felt about that.

The smiles say it all. Jonjo O'Neill welcomes his Royal Ascot winner Gypsy Fiddler (above), and celebrates with Dawn Run's owner Charmian Hill after collecting his Cheltenham Gold Cup trophy (below).

Peter Scudamore

The record books have been rewritten since Peter Scudamore gave new meaning to the jump jockeys' statistics, thanks to his partnership with Martin Pipe.

Statistics can be manipulated to prove almost any point, but not in Peter Scudamore's case. The figures add up to only one thing, the biggest collection of records in the history of National Hunt racing.

The fastest 50 winners in a season, the fastest 100, the most winners in a season, and the most winners by any jump jockey: they all belong to Scudamore, who in 1992 also stands to become holder of the outright record of eight jockeys' championships.

It was not always so. Born in June 1958, the son of noted jump jockey Michael Scudamore, he took three years – until 31 August 1978 – to ride his first winner under Rules as an amateur. But once he turned professional with David Nicholson's stable in 1979, the momentum began to build.

Another record falls to Peter Scudamore and Arden becomes winner No. 1,139 to beat John Francome's total.

Even then his early seasons were seriously interrupted by injury – a fractured skull cut short his championship challenge to John Francome in 1981, and a broken arm the following year cost him the overall title, with Francome sportingly surrendering a share. Only when Francome retired in April 1985 did Scudamore emerge into the limelight and he has taken every jockeys' championship since.

Riding for Nicholson, Fred and Mary Rimell and John Edwards, Scudamore enjoyed a number of big-race wins, including a Cheltenham Festival double in 1986 on Broadsword (Triumph Hurdle) and Charter Party (NH Handicap Chase). These were the first winners at jump racing's premier meeting for both Nicholson, who was brought up near the course, and Scudamore; ironically they were the last they shared, for the partnership split up shortly afterwards and a year later Scudamore joined Fred Winter.

The move proved to be highly significant in Scudamore's career, though not for the obvious reason that it provided the connection, later carried on by Charlie Brooks, which brought him a Champion Hurdle victory in 1988 on Celtic Shot. The twist was that it gave him scope to build on an association that had begun on 2 March 1985.

History will reveal that the real turning point for Scudamore came that afternoon at Haydock, where he won the opening

Martin Pipe keeps note (left), while Peter Scudamore gets down to the business of winning races (above), here riding Bajan Sunshine.

novices' hurdle on Hieronymous, trained by Martin Pipe. The *Raceform* comment about the winner is more than a little prophetic: 'made all, soon well clear, hit 7th and 3 out, stayed on'. Many of the hundreds of subsequent winners from this quarter have shown similar qualities, forcing the pace, making light of occasional errors and pounding the opposition into the ground just when it seemed they would capitulate.

It is impossible to say who has been better for the other, Scudamore or Pipe. The truth is that they complement each other, with a partnership based on a high work rate and even higher professionalism. Scudamore has made an art out of cutting down the risks, and while other jockeys may be more stylish, none is a better judge of pace or stronger in a finish.

It was Pipe's ammunition, fired from his stable on the Devon–Somerset border, which enabled Scudamore to register the fastest 50 in October 1989, the fastest 100 in December 1988, the highest number of winners in a season, 221 in 1988–89, and the most winners by a jump jockey, 1,139 on 18 November 1989. It also took him to the height of 1,500 winners on 3 March 1992. But numbers are not all, and together they have set about lifting the quality of winners with such as Bonanza Boy, Sabin du Loir, Strands of Gold, Chatam, Rolling Ball and Carvill's Hill.

Undemonstrative yet articulate and approachable, Scudamore is a marvellous ambassador for National Hunt racing. He has achieved statistical domination without losing the admiration of his colleagues; and no one would begrudge him the remaining pieces in his personal jigsaw, the Cheltenham Gold Cup and Grand National.

Great Owners and Trainers

Nowhere in British racing have there been greater changes over the last 25 years than in the ranks of owners and trainers. Some names have stayed the course; more have dropped out or been forced to accept different circumstances. Many of the newcomers represent a different outlook from the previous generation.

The days of the large-scale, British-based owner-breeder seem to be numbered, and Jim Joel's death earlier this year severed another important link. Some press on with fewer horses but equally high hopes of hitting the jackpot, and the return to prominence of Robert Sangster, after a short lull, shows that all needn't be lost if the arrow misses the target once or twice.

Sangster, who dominated the late 1970s had to bow before the new wave of Arab owners in the 1980s but he has adjusted his aim and is back among the big guns. Others may have to follow suit, for the major Arab owners show no signs of weakening their resolve to be involved in the highest class whether in breeding, or owning, or both.

Generally reserved, quiet and polite men they have brought dignity in their domination. Theirs is the biggest change to the spread of ownership in the last 25 years when costs have escalated and outside jump racing it is hard – but not impossible – to find a bargain.

With the Arab owners has come a boost for a number of established trainers and a chance for the new breed. The newcomers are still making their mark, but the effect on the careers of longer-established trainers will become obvious in the following pages.

GREAT OWNERS

Every owner wants to win the Derby or Grand National. A few are lucky enough to achieve the ultimate goal, but most have to go on trying. Among those who carry on the search for success at the highest level are businessmen, Arab princes – and even British royalty.

Times change, and nowhere in British horseracing has the emphasis switched so much in the last 25 years as in ownership.

At the beginning of the period under review it was virtually guaranteed that whoever raced the Derby winner would end the year as leading owner. That was the case in 1966, when Lady Zia Wernher topped the win-money list by sole virtue of Charlottown's victories in the Derby (worth £74,489) and the Oxfordshire Stakes (£3,585).

It was also the case in 1968, when Raymond Guest headed the table on the strength of one horse, Sir Ivor. But come 1979, when Sir Michael Sobell was leading British owner, the picture had already started to change. Sobell's winners of 13 races for almost £340,000 included the Derby hero Troy, but since his colt also won the King George VI and Queen Elizabeth Diamond Stakes and Benson and Hedges Gold Cup, it was clear Sobell owed his position to the proliferation of valuable races.

Ever the enthusiast, Jim Joel greets Ballyhane at Sandown Park.

However, winning the Derby is still the major aim of most racehorse owners, and in 1967 Royal Palace etched the name of **Jim Joel** on the roll of honour. Twenty years later he completed a rarely achieved double when his Maori Venture won the Grand National.

Born Harry Joel Joel, he appeared on the race cards as H J Joel but was known as Jim throughout the 50 years he was involved in racing, where his black and scarlet colours stood out both summer and winter. Apart from Royal Palace, his best Flat horses in this period were the Classic winners Fairy Footsteps and Light Cavalry, and Song, Welsh Pageant and Connaught. His other good National Hunt horses included Buona notte, Beau Normand, The Laird, Summerville and Door Latch.

Modest, kind, and generous in both victory and defeat, he died in March 1992 at the age of 97.

Joel represented the longest link in modern racing. As a significant owner-breeder he belonged to the old school; the man who closely followed him as leading owner in 1969, **David Robinson**, was from the new.

Robinson had won the 2,000 Guineas with Our Babu in 1955, but it was in 1967, helped by a fortune made from television rentals, that he became Britain's biggest owner. At his peak he had 120 horses and three private trainers.

Two-year-olds and sprinters fitted his bill, especially when they could be sold on as stallions, and having graded his horses to match the categories of racecourses, he instructed his trainers to make the most of the opportunities. Winning races was the objective, and in 1973 he set a record for an owner with 115 winners totalling £114,735, though it was not sufficient to make him leading owner for money won.

Yellow God, My Swallow, Deep Diver, So Blessed, Tudor Music, Green God and Bitty Girl were smart sprinters who starred for him in the top races, while the St Leger second Meadowville was his best stayer.

Ill-health forced Robinson to cut down his interests from 1975 and he had his last winner in 1978. No one but his closest associates knew what made him tick, for he refused, politely, to give interviews. His tactics were not always welcomed by other owners and trainers, and his criticism of the Jockey Club – later toned down – did not endear him to traditionalists. But those who worked for him enjoyed good conditions.

Robinson signalled the start of the business age, and it was carried onward and upward by **Robert Sangster**, the Vernons football pools heir who with the help of a few close associates changed the face of racing in Britain and internationally.

Sangster's game plan, once established in the mid-1970s, was simple in principle: buy top-class prospects at the yearling sales in the United States, race them in the highest class, and make the most of the best as stallions. In practice, and aided largely by the skill of trainer Vincent O'Brien and jockeys Lester Piggott and Pat Eddery, it paid off in a big way.

Five times in the nine years between 1977 and 1984 Sangster was leading owner in Britain, often sharing his exploits with syndicate members. He won the Derby with The Minstrel and Golden Fleece; the 2,000 Guineas with Lomond and El Gran Senor; the Dewhurst Stakes with The Minstrel, Try My Best, Monteverdi, Storm Bird and El Gran Senor; and the Benson and Hedges Gold Cup with Hawaiian Sound, Assert and Caerleon. In France he won the Derby with Assert and Caerleon, and the Prix de l'Arc de Triomphe with Alleged (twice) and Detroit; and in Ireland he won the Sweeps Derby with The Minstrel, Assert and El Gran Senor.

Robert Sangster (right) and trainer Barry Hills are passing on last-minute riding arrangements, or perhaps just passing the time of day with their jockey.

At one stage Sangster's bloodstock interests, masterminded from his home on the Isle of Man, stretched from England, Ireland, France, Germany and Italy to Australia, New Zealand, the States and South Africa. But his domination was soon to be challenged, and he changed tack, rationalizing his buying and breeding operation, and purchasing the old-established Manton estate in Wiltshire, where he installed Michael Dickinson as private trainer.

Though the stable was transformed, the venture was ill-starred and Dickinson was

relieved of the job within a year. He was replaced by Barry Hills, but he too moved out within a short time as Sangster sought to realize his assets by selling the estate. No buyer came forward; Sangster set up his stepson-in-law Peter Chapple-Hyam for the 1991 season and the result was an amazing return to prominence for his green, blue and white colours. With the help of his other trainers Sangster had 54 winners in Britain, including three smart two-year-olds in Rodrigo de Triano, winner of the Champagne Stakes and Middle Park Stakes, Dr Devious and the filly Musicale.

One threat to Sangster's domination came from the **Aga Khan**, who had begun restoring his family's racing fortunes following their decline on the untimely death of his father, Aly Khan, in 1960. The Aga Khan started the process in 1973, and gave recovery a huge push in the space of a year when he bought the Dupre and Boussac bloodstock interests.

Luca Cumani applauds, the Aga Khan looks on, after winning the Derby with Kahyasi.

Here was a new empire shored up by purchases but built on the old principle of astutely using its own resources. Basing his training on a complex freshly built at Chantilly and signing up Yves Saint-Martin as stable jockey, the Aga Khan put the family's chocolate and green colours back in the headlines by winning the French Derby with Top Ville, Darshaan, Mouktar and Natroun between 1979 and 1987, as well as the Prix de l'Arc de Triomphe with Akiyda.

In 1979, after an absence of 15 years, the Aga Khan had horses trained in Britain, and along came the Derby winners Shergar (1981), Shahrastani (1986) and Kahyasi (1988). Shergar's success helped the Aga Khan to become leading owner.

Then, in December 1990, came a dramatic withdrawal from England, brought about by the Aga Khan's dispute with the Jockey Club over a positive post-race test taken from Aliysa, who was disqualified after she had won the Oaks in 1989. It was not the first time the Aga Khan had found reason to question the Jockey Club's scientific methods, but on this occasion, as well as protesting loud and long, he took telling action. First resigning from the Jockey Club itself, he removed his 90 horses trained in England and sent them to France and Ireland, vowing never to have another runner in England until the authorities changed their veterinary operations. So far he has kept his word.

The loss of the Aga Khan's interest was significant, but there was already in existence a more powerful challenge to the likes of Robert Sangster. It had emerged from the Middle East in the form of the Maktoum family from Dubai and Khalid Abdullah from Saudi Arabia.

The **Maktoum brothers** – Maktoum, Hamdan, Mohammed and Ahmed – rule oil-rich Dubai. Sheikh Mohammed had his first runner, Hatta, in Britain in 1977, when she won four races including the Molecomb Stakes. Maktoum Al-Maktoum had his first winner, Shaab, in 1979, and Hamdan Al-Maktoum his first, Mushref, in 1980. Sheikh Ahmed, the youngest brother, was persuaded into ownership slightly later; his first horse, Wassl, won the Irish 2,000 Guineas in 1984.

Within the space of a dozen years the family interest, grown to include a number of cousins and close associates, has developed the biggest collection of horses ever seen in this country, split among several trainers. They have expanded to Ireland, France, the United States and Australia, and each of the three elder brothers has at least two studs in Britain,

Ireland and the States. Their further support extends to sponsoring major races, huge donations to racing charities and, in Sheikh Mohammed's case, backing a daily newspaper, the *Racing Post*. Hundreds of people have benefited directly from their involvement; others believe they have suffered from their widespread domination.

In the early stages the Maktoums' empire was built around purchases at the yearling sales. Money was no object and Sheikh Mohammed was responsible for two major records – $10.2 million for the abject failure Snaafi Dancer, a world record until broken by Robert Sangster at $13.1 million for Seattle Dancer; and 2,588,000 guineas, a European record, for Authaal, who won the Irish St Leger before continuing his racing

Hamdan Al-Maktoum (above) has a Gold Cup win to cheer him on a rainy day at Royal Ascot.

Racing has always attracted royal families. Khalid Abdullah, from Saudi Arabia, receives the owner's trophy for Dancing Brave's win in the Prix de l'Arc de Triomphe (left).

career in Australia. More recently the Maktoums' own thoroughbred breeding has come to the fore.

Inevitably, more of their horses fail to win than are successful, but the triumphs have been far-reaching, with Sheikh Mohammed – who won a record 176 races on the Flat in Britain in 1990 – leading owner for money won six times out of seven between 1985 and 1991, and Hamdan Al-Maktoum top on the only other occasion.

Hamdan remains the only brother to have won the Derby, with Nashwan, who also won the 2,000 Guineas. His other British Classic winners are Salsabil (1,000 Guineas and Oaks), Shadayid (1,000 Guineas) and Touching Wood (St Leger). Sheikh Mohammed has won the 1,000 Guineas with Oh So Sharp and Musical Bliss; the Oaks with Oh So Sharp, Unite and Diminuendo; and the St Leger with Oh So Sharp. Maktoum's British Classic winners are Ma Biche and Hatoof (1,000 Guineas), Shadeed (2,000 Guineas) and Jet Ski Lady (Oaks). Sheikh Ahmed's best winner has been Mtoto.

None of the Maktoum brothers has yet won the Prix de l'Arc de Triomphe, but that jewel in the European crown has twice fallen to **Khalid Abdullah**, with Rainbow Quest, who was awarded the 1985 race on the demotion of Sagace, and Dancing Brave, who avenged his Derby defeat in 1986. Abdullah also has a Derby victory to his name, with Quest For Fame, but he has yet to be champion owner in Britain, twice finishing runner-up.

Like most of his Arab counterparts, Abdullah is a very private man. He too started in Britain in a small way, with a few horses trained in small stables in 1978. Two years later he became the first Arab to own a British Classic winner when Known Fact was awarded the 2,000 Guineas on the disqualification of Nureyev.

Less inclined to spend huge sums, and a little more inclined to keep his colts in training longer, Abdullah has had other top-class wins in this country through Toulon (St Leger), Warning (Sussex and Queen Elizabeth II Stakes), Rousillon, the sprinters Dowsing and Danehill, and Bakharoff.

The only major Arab owner attracted to any great extent to National Hunt racing has been Sheikh Ali Abu Khamsin, who had most of his horses with the Rimells and Fred Winter, and was leading owner over jumps for five seasons out of six at the start of the 1980s.

Though prize money has blossomed and the number of major sponsored jump races has increased in the last 25 years, the Cheltenham Gold Cup and Grand National still stand out, and whichever owner wins either has an even-money chance of leading the championship. The **Queen Mother** is unlikely to reach those heights – she would have been leading owner had Devon Loch added his name to Grand National folklore in 1956 – but she remains the sport's greatest ambassador. Magnanimous in defeat, charming in victory, she has been a fervent supporter since her first horse, Monaveen, won in October 1949.

The Queen Mother, National Hunt's most popular owner, and the Princess of Wales share transport at Royal Ascot.

GREAT TRAINERS

Old school or new wave: racehorse trainers have reached the top from different directions, with different approaches. For some the business has been in the family for years; for others it was a case of starting from scratch and hang tradition.

When 1966 dawned, Ireland's senior trainer Paddy Prendergast had been champion trainer in Britain for three successive years; Ian Balding and Dick Hern were second and third in the table; Noel Murless was still at the top of the tree after almost 20 years there; Harry Wragg was setting out for Europe with his top horses – and the list of leading owners was a mix of British and American names, with a Frenchman topping the 1965 chart by virtue of owning the Derby winner.

As 1992 awakes, the Irish are struggling to match the best in Europe; Balding and Hern have been joined by the fresh blood of such as Paul Cole, Richard Hannon, Michael Stoute, Clive Brittain, John Dunlop, Barry Hills and Luca Cumani; Henry Cecil, who succeeded his father-in-law Noel Murless, has been champion trainer nine times in the last 16 seasons; forays from Britain to the Continent and far beyond are commonplace – and Arab owners dominate, while the French rarely venture outside their own boundary.

Master trainer Noel Murless surveys the scene on Newmarket Heath.

Noel Murless, who was based in Yorkshire and Wiltshire before moving to Newmarket in 1952, had trained ten Classic winners by the end of 1965; he was to add nine more before he retired in the autumn of 1976. Quiet but firm, kind but never one to suffer fools gladly, he was a master at being ready for the big occasion without using the racecourse in preparation, and he always put his horses first.

Leading trainer nine times between 1948 and 1973, he set his third record for winning prize-money in a season in 1967, when Busted won the Eclipse Stakes and the King George VI and Queen Elizabeth Stakes, and Royal Palace the 2,000 Guineas and Derby. The following year Royal Palace won the Eclipse Stakes and King George VI and Queen Elizabeth Stakes.

Murless, knighted in 1977, died in May 1987, aged 77. Lester Piggott described his biggest attributes as patience and insight, and he should know. Murless appointed Piggott to succeed Sir Gordon Richards as his stable jockey in 1954, at the age of 19, and they were together until 1966.

An old partnership (above), between trainer Vincent O'Brien and jockey Lester Piggott, discusses tactics, and a new one (right), between Henry Cecil and his second wife Natalie, takes time out at Newmarket.

They broke up when Piggott decided to ride Valoris instead of Murless's Varinia in the 1966 Oaks. Piggott was proved right; he won on Valoris and, after a short time freelancing, he began to ride regularly for that filly's trainer, **Vincent O'Brien**. So began another chapter in the remarkable story of Ireland's premier trainer.

O'Brien, based at Ballydoyle in Co. Tipperary, had already swept everything before him in the National Hunt world when he turned to the Flat in the 1950s. Ballymoss was his first top-class horse, but the turning-point came in 1966, and though the appearance of Piggott may have been nothing more than a fortunate coincidence, it surely did no harm.

O'Brien was leading trainer in Britain for the first time in 1966, when he won the 1,000 Guineas with Glad Rags and the Oaks with Valoris, and the Eclipse Stakes with Pieces of Eight. He has added only one win-money championship to the record, in 1977, when The Minstrel's wins in the Derby and the King George VI and Queen Elizabeth Stakes were largely responsible. But that tells only a fraction of the story, for O'Brien has sent over comparatively few runners and all have been aimed at the richest prizes.

His achievements are better judged from the other star names he has dispatched to Britain and France from his magnificent training establishment near Cashel – Sir Ivor, Nijinsky, Roberto, Apalachee, Alleged, Thatching, Storm Bird, Golden Fleece, Lomond, El Gran Senor, Caerleon, Sadler's Wells and Law Society.

The last six years have not been so successful; a virus, the competing force of Arab owners and a downturn in bloodstock values have seen to that, and the flop of the syndicate company Classic Thoroughbreds, on which O'Brien relied heavily, has not helped. The way has been left for other Irish trainers to make their mark, helped by an influx of Arab and American owners. Dermot Weld and Jim Bolger have made most progress, vying for the biggest number of wins in a season and targeting the top races, but even they would admit that O'Brien's star is still out of reach.

When Lester Piggott ended his association with O'Brien in 1980, he was back in familiar surroundings within a year. He joined **Henry Cecil** at the Newmarket stables where he had served Noel Murless, and in 1981 was champion jockey for the first time in ten years. That was the influence of Cecil, stepson of the outstanding Royal trainer Sir Cecil Boyd-Rochfort and the most successful British trainer of the 1980s. Since Cecil was champion for the first time in 1976, no other trainer has won more races or more money. His score of 180 wins in 1987, for £1.88 million in win-money alone, broke a British record which had stood for over a century.

Once regarded as a reckless young man, he settled quickly and responsibly into the job of training and pursues his aims with diligence and care which belie his outwardly casual approach. A meticulous planner, he rarely goes racing except on major occasions, preferring to concentrate on work at home. His distate for travelling seemed to be translated to his horses, but more recently he has been prepared to race them overseas, with good results.

He has won 13 British Classics, from Bolkonski in the 2,000 Guineas in 1975 to Michelozzo in the St Leger in 1989, including four out of five with Oh So Sharp and Slip Anchor in Cauthen's first year, 1985. Slip Anchor and Reference Point are his two Derby winners, while he won the French and Irish equivalents with Old Vic.

Though he has trained four champion two-year-olds – Wollow, Diesis, Reference Point and High Estate – he relies on patience to produce smart three-year-olds, and is equally adept with fillies (Indian Skimmer, Diminuendo and One In a Million being in or around the class of Oh So Sharp), milers (Kris, Bolkonski, Diesis and Wollow being the best) and stayers (Le Moss, Ardross and Buckskin standing out).

Until Generous helped Paul Cole break the sequence in 1991, only two trainers have loosened Cecil's championship stranglehold since 1978. **Dick Hern**, who had headed the list in 1962 and 1972, was top again in 1980, the year of Ela-Mana-Mou, Henbit and Bireme, and 1983, when Sun Princess was the star. **Michael Stoute** was the leader in 1981, 1986 and 1989.

With 13 years' start, Dick Hern has won two British Classics more than Cecil, 15 in all. They begin with Hethersett, when he was private trainer to Lionel Holliday, in the St Leger in 1962, and run through to the 2,000 Guineas and Derby of Nashwan, for his latest principal patron, Hamdan Al-Maktoum, in 1989. Brigadier Gerard, Troy and Nashwan are hard to separate as the best horses trained by Hern; while such as Bustino, Petoski, Sallust, Relkino, Dunfermline, Highest Hopes and Highclere would run the other big-race winners close.

Respect for Hern, one of the old school of publicity-avoiding trainers, is based on his skill and loyalty – he has had only two retained jockeys, Joe Mercer and Willie Carson, since 1963. It has been sharpened by a hunting accident in December 1984 which

Big-race trophies are forgotten for the moment as the Queen chats to her former trainer Dick Hern.

Michael Stoute has been going only one way since he started training in Newmarket, and that's to the top.

eventually put him in a wheelchair for the rest of his life, further ill-health, and the final blow, a strong feeling that he was shabbily treated when asked to vacate his West Ilsley stables, owned by the Queen, at the end of 1989.

Michael Stoute was born in Barbados and arrived in England in 1965 to work for Pat Rohan in Yorkshire. He followed three years in the north with a similar period in Newmarket, learning the ropes, before he set out on his own in 1972. He began with 15 horses, and in his second season won the Stewards' Cup with Alphadamus and the Ayr Gold Cup with Blue Cashmere, both cheaply bought as yearlings.

He won his first Classic, the Oaks, with Fair Salinia in 1978, but the turning-point was 1981, the year Walter Swinburn joined as stable jockey and, more to the point, the year of Shergar and champion sprinter Marwell.

The arrival of Shergar's owner the Aga Khan was as crucial to Stoute as the appearance of Sheikh Mohammed and Maktoum Al-Maktoum on his list of patrons. The Aga Khan left him Shahrastani (the 1986 Derby hero) and Doyoun, whom he turned into Classic winners; Aliysa, a Classic winner in all but the record books; and Shardari and Shernazar.

Outlasting the Aga Khan, the Maktoum brothers have gone even further. Sheikh Mohammed has owned Musical Bliss, Unite, Shaadi, Sonic Lady and Melodist, all Classic winners in Britain or Ireland, as well as Ajdal, champion sprinter in 1987, and Zilzal, Horse of the Year in 1989. Maktoum Al-Maktoum had the Irish Derby winner Shareef Dancer in the stable.

An all-round sportsman with a passion for cricket, Stoute can be intense or amusingly affable, depending on the needs of the moment, but he is never less than passionate about all aspects of training. Winning the Triumph Hurdle and Champion Hurdle with Kribensis probably gave him as much pleasure as any of his seven British Classics (eight, counting Aliysa).

Stoute's loss of the Aga Khan's horses has been, in part, France's gain, as has been the recent decision by some prominent Arab owners to divert to Chantilly horses which might have been trained in England. Two of the best established French trainers, Criquette Head and François Boutin, have been among the chief beneficiaries.

Criquette Head is the latest in a famous Anglo-French family of trainers. She follows her grandfather Willie, her father Alec and her uncle Peter. Her brother Freddy has been one of France's top jockeys for more than 20 years. Alec Head, who finished second in the Champion Hurdle during his riding days, enjoyed enormous success in Britain between 1954 and 1960, but his runners became scarcer and his last big-race winners in this country were Mige in the 1968 Cheveley Park Stakes and Green Dancer in the 1974 William Hill Futurity.

By the time Alec Head retired in 1984, aged 60, to concentrate on his extensive breeding interests in France and the United States, his daughter had begun training and

France has been well served by its top trainers Alec and Criquette Head (left), and François Boutin (below)

had won the Prix de l'Arc de Triomphe with Three Troikas (owned by her mother and ridden by her brother) and the Cheveley Park Stakes and 1,000 Guineas with Ma Biche. Once given the family field to herself, she has maintained its superb record. She emulated her father, who won the French Derby with Lavandin, when Bering took the premier French Classic in 1986, and might have gone halfway towards his record of four Arc wins had Bering not been injured when he finished second to Dancing Brave. She has, however, outstripped her father in the 1,000 Guineas by gaining further successes in the race with Ravinella and Hatoof.

The brother–sister combination split up at the end of 1986 but only because Freddy was lured away by **François Boutin**, to ride for one of the only two stables in France bigger than Head's. The arrangement lasted for four years, during which they chiefly shared in the brilliance of the filly Miesque, winner of the English and French 1,000 Guineas and two Breeders' Cup Miles.

Having been assistant to Etienne Pollet, Boutin began training in a very small way in 1965, but there was no doubt about his level of ambition. It quickly became obvious to British racegoers when he won the Oaks in 1968 with La Lagune, who, despite the unfamiliar background of her trainer, started favourite. Since then he has been the most regular French visitor to Britain, even putting behind him the disappointments of Nureyev's disqualification for interference in the 2,000 Guineas and Trepan's dual disqualification after traces of banned substances were found following his wins in the Prince of Wales's Stakes and the Eclipse Stakes.

On the brighter side, he has also won the 2,000 Guineas with Nonoalco and Zino, the Champion Stakes with Flossy and Northern Baby, and the Gold Cup at Ascot three times in a row with the magnificent Sagaro. In France he has won most major races, except the Arc, including the Derby with Caracolero.

Boutin prefers to leave spoken English to others – though he seems to understand everything he is asked in English – but it did not stop him attracting plenty of attention from outside France with his early success, and today he runs the most international stable in Europe. England is just one of his European staging-posts; top races in Ireland, Italy, Germany and beyond have fallen to his meticulous planning. In the United States, where he first made people take notice by winning two Turf Classics and a Washington DC International with April Run, race followers readily remember Miesque and they are still talking about his latest Breeders' Cup triumph with Arazi.

The Breeders' Cup, the import of yearlings from the Kentucky Sales, and the export of good-class British-trained horses to further their careers has brought racing in the United States into sharper focus in recent years. It has also made familiar the names of Charlie Whittingham and D Wayne Lukas, arguably the two best trainers in America – allowing that Jack van Berg has won more races than either and Woody Stephens had trained more divisional champions until Lukas arrived.

Charlie Whittingham belongs to the old school, and not simply because he is a veteran, having been born in 1913 and a trainer since 1934. Having learnt his trade with the great Horatio Luro, he has made his reputation with slower maturing horses, and his astounding success with older horses imported from Europe is no coincidence. Even his own career can be said to have been a slow-burner, for though he had his first major stakes winner in 1953, he became champion trainer for the first of seven times in 1970 and trained his first

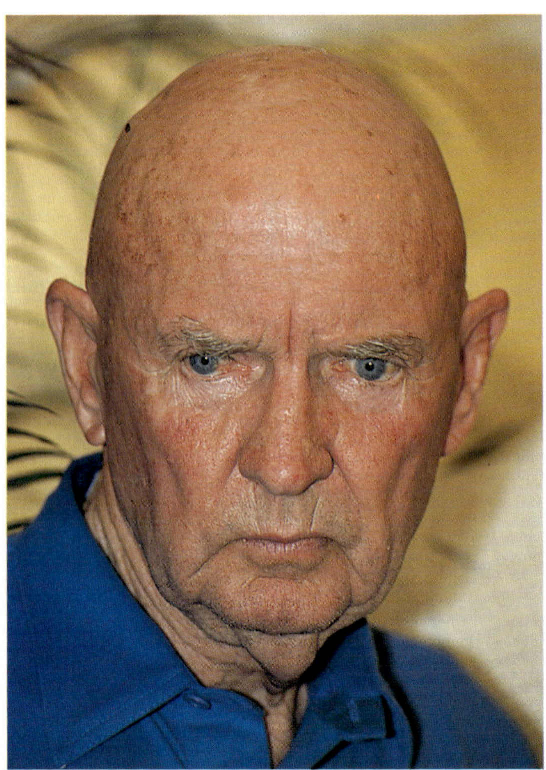

Charlie Whittingham, the Bald Eagle, has a knack for bringing out the best in older horses, especially those sent to the States from Europe.

Horse of the Year, Ack Ack, the following year.

Based in California and aided by Bill Shoemaker, he really came into his own in the 1980s. In 1982 he became the first trainer to win $4 million in a year, and then he struck out as the oldest trainer to win the Kentucky Derby, with his second and third Horses of the Year, Ferdinand in 1986 and Sunday Silence three years later. Each went on to win the Breeders' Cup Classic and vies with Ack Ack as the best horse he has trained.

D Wayne Lukas, born in 1935, is from the new school, a university graduate who coached basketball before he graduated into the thoroughbred scene full-time in 1978 via quarter-horse training. He plays for big stakes at the yearling sales and even bigger stakes on the racecourse, and his turnover of horses reflects his thirst for success.

He has quenched it in amazing fashion: leading trainer for prize money every year from 1983; the same for races won from 1987; the first trainer to win stakes totalling eight figures in a season, in 1984; the winner of a record $17.8 million in 1988; the trainer of a record 14 divisional champions; the first to win more stakes money in a year than the country's leading jockey; and winner of ten Breeders' Cup races and placed in 16 others.

A ready talker, when his hectic schedule allows him to be pinned down, he attributes his success to preparing his horses mentally as well as physically.

If Australia had been a little closer, and European horses had gone out there in sufficient numbers to guarantee publicity, the name of **Colin Hayes** might have been as familiar as that of Whittingham or Lukas. It deserves to be, for Hayes ranks alongside any trainer in the world. Like Whittingham, he has brought the best out of imports from the northern hemisphere, winning the famed Melbourne Cup with Beldale Ball for Robert Sangster in 1980 and with At Talaq for Hamdan Al-Maktoum in 1986. Like Lukas, he has set new standards of success for his own country.

Hayes built his reputation from nothing. He began with one horse shortly after the War, and after six years won his first trainers' championship in Adelaide. When he retired in July 1990, to hand over to his son David, he had won 28 Adelaide titles, as well as 13 in Melbourne, not to mention 14 state Derbys, 11 state Oaks, and just about every worthwhile race in the Australian calendar. And he did it from a magnificent, spacious training establishment, Lindsay Park at Angaston in South Australia, which he also built from nothing. There he developed his plan to control the cycle from breeding to foaling to racing and back to breeding.

Hayes retired with a world record to his name; his ten winners on 23 January 1982 add up to the most by one trainer on the Flat in a single day. The highest number ever won by a trainer is 12, which **Michael Dickinson** achieved over jumps from his 21 runners on six British courses on 27 December 1982.

Attention to detail and careful planning were the hallmarks of former champion amateur rider Dickinson in a training career over jumps that was as brilliant as it was brief. He took over the licence from his father Tony in 1980, trained for four seasons and was champion three times. In all he won 374 races, including a British record of 120 in 1982–83, the season he was responsible for the first five finishers in the Cheltenham Gold Cup.

Colin Hayes oversees the whole thoroughbred cycle at Lindsay Park.

Dickinson only rarely saddled a runner which did not have a realistic chance of winning. His record total of 120 came from 259 races, and included 30 first-time-out winners from 57 individual runners. To make the achievement even more outstanding, he won some of the season's most highly prized and competitive steeplechases – the Hennessy Cognac Gold Cup and Cheltenham Gold Cup with Bregawn; SGB Chase with Captain John; King George VI Chase with Wayward Lad; Edward Hanmer Chase with Silver Buck; Peter Marsh Chase with Ashley House; Queen Mother Champion Chase with Badsworth Boy; and Greenall Whitley Chase with Righthand Man.

Preparing this squad, of which Silver Buck also won the Cheltenham Gold Cup in 1982, was meat and drink to Dickinson, and his ill-starred venture as private trainer to Robert Sangster and subsequent departure for the United States takes nothing away from his achievements.

When Dickinson left home for a career on the Flat, that allowed **Fred Winter** to put his name to the jump trainers' title for a record eighth and final time. His previous seven had been clocked in the eight seasons between 1970 and 1978, when he won most of the major races he had not won as a jockey, and a great many in which he could now claim dual success.

As jockey and trainer, Fred Winter was supreme in the National Hunt business.

There has never been a more successful all-rounder in National Hunt racing than Fred Winter, whose total of four jockeys' championships would have been greater but for injury, and whose reputation for honesty and integrity could not have been bettered. He retired from riding in April 1964 and, having had his application to become a starter turned down by the Jockey Club, started training at Lambourn.

From the start, Winter the trainer was a resounding success. In his first season he won the Grand National with Jay Trump, and in his second he won it with Anglo. It seemed it would be difficult to match that, but in the four seasons between 1971 and 1974 he won the Champion Hurdle three times, with Bula (twice) and Lanzarote, and in 1978 he won the Cheltenham Gold Cup with Midnight Court. Pendil, twice winner of the King George VI Chase, was another stable star, and the Australian import Crisp excelled in defeat when beaten less than a length by Red Rum in the Grand National, where he was conceding 23lb.

Winter's last big winner was Plundering in the 1986 Whitbread Gold Cup. The following year he fractured his skull in a fall at his home and he never fully recovered. His assistant Charlie Brooks took over the stable.

If Fred Winter can be described as the best all-rounder in National Hunt, **David Elsworth** deserves to be called Britain's best all-round trainer of the moment, full stop. But it was not always that way; he was 39 before he started training under his own name.

He had been in racing for more than 20 years, as stable lad, journeyman jump jockey and assistant trainer, but had also spent six years doing a variety of other jobs after one employer fell foul of Jockey Club Rules. And when he did start in 1979 it was with a handful of horses, though he won the Great Metropolitan Handicap in each of his first two seasons. Upward mobility really began when he moved to Whitsbury in 1982.

One of the least pretentious members of the training profession, Elsworth will always be associated with Desert Orchid, but the breadth of success established in his first seasons at Whitsbury has been built on, and he has shown himself as capable of producing high-class sprinters (Indian Ridge and Lugana Beach), two-year-olds (Dead Certain and Seattle Rhyme) and fillies (In the Groove and Miss Silca Key) as hurdlers (Heighlin and Oh So Risky) and chasers (the Grand National winner Rhyme 'N' Reason as well as his famous grey).

Elsworth has been champion jumps trainer once, in 1987–88, squeezing in just before **Martin Pipe** arrived on the scene and

Every trainer needs to use his eyes and ears. David Elsworth (left) watches his string of horses as Desert Orchid leads them back to base, while (below) Martin Pipe passes on the news that Chatam has won the Hennessy.

started rewriting the record books. When Pipe became the first man to train two hundred winners in a jumps season in 1988–89, a racing newspaper suggested the record might never be beaten. It was, the following season, by Pipe – and in 1990–91, again by Pipe, and again with an increased score, this time 230 winners.

Son of a bookmaker, Pipe has turned dedication and application into a string of National Hunt records: the fastest 50 and 100 winners in a season; the most winners; the most prize money; the first trainer to win more than £1 million; and a share of a British record with five winners at a single fixture.

Pipe is unique in having won at least one hundred races for each of the last six jumps seasons, but having formerly relied almost entirely on quantity and low-grade races in the early stages, he has lifted his standards by more than a notch.

With superb modern training facilities, an on-site vet and careful attention to scientific detail, Pipe has brought a fresh approach to training. He has also attracted a degree of envy and suspicion in addition to admiration. In some respects he is the West Country's answer to D Wayne Lukas.

27
GOLDEN
MINSTREL

Great Races

Great Races need not involve Great Horses, Great Jockeys, or even Great Owners and Trainers. It all depends how one defines a Great Race.

Is it one you remember because you were there and the occasion was memorable? Or was it because the housekeeping money was in the balance but everything came right in the end?

Is it one that involves a favourite horse in a favourite race, or a special jockey? Or is it simply one that sticks in the mind, for whatever reason?

With so much material to choose from, the easiest way out of the dilemma was to pick one from each year, starting with 1966 because that brought the great Arkle into the scope.

Every race in the collection has a special significance. It might involve a horse worthy of the occasion, such as Vaguely Noble, or an incident that everyone will remember, such as the twenty-third fence pile-up in Foinavon's Grand National.

It might be the start of a great run, such as Red Rum's first Grand National, or it might be the end of one, as in Sagaro's last Gold Cup at Royal Ascot. It might be a moment of controversy, such as Nureyev's disqualification in the 2,000 Guineas, or one of celebration, as in Michael Dickinson's first five finishers in the Cheltenham Gold Cup.

It might be the climax to a marvellous achievement, as when Provideo equalled the record for wins by a two-year-old, or the beginning of an adventure, as in the first race on an all-weather surface.

Whatever it is, it's there for a reason – good, bad or indifferent.

CHELTENHAM GOLD CUP, 1966

Won by Arkle – Thursday 17 March

Arkle was unique. He was so good they changed the Rules to give the rest a chance, so that when he was entered for a handicap, two sets of weights were framed – one with Arkle in it, and one without him. When he did run in a handicap at his peak, he always carried much more weight than the other runners, but the range from 12st 7lb to 9st 7lb was still not enough to give more than a handful a chance of beating him.

Arkle gets away with the biggest mistake of his career at the eleventh fence in the 1966 Cheltenham Gold Cup.

Weight did beat Arkle; for instance, in the 1964 Massey-Ferguson Gold Cup he carried 12st 10lb and went down by about a length to two cracking good chasers in Flying Wild and Buona notte, who were saddled with 32lb and 26lb less respectively. And in the 1966 Hennessy Gold Cup he carried 12st 7lb and failed by half a length to concede 35lb to Stalbridge Colonist. Considering the Hennessy winner went on to finish third under 11st 6lb in the Massey-Ferguson and was beaten less than a length in the Cheltenham Gold Cup, it was a phenomenal effort by Arkle.

The nature of the National Hunt programme at this time meant there were two choices for Arkle, either he tackled handicaps or he stayed home in Ireland until the King George VI Chase and Cheltenham Gold Cup came round. Owner Anne, Duchess of Westminster, and trainer Tom Dreaper took the option to run, and Arkle became a legend.

His great English-trained rival Mill House had one early verdict over him, in the 1963 Hennessy Gold Cup, but it was not long before it became apparent which was the master. Though Mill House started odds-on favourite for the Cheltenham Gold Cup in 1964, Arkle beat him by five lengths, and the following year he stretched the margin to 20 lengths to prove beyond all doubt that he was one of the greatest chasers

The familiar Arkle jumping style, as he takes the water at Ascot.

of all time. Only Golden Miller could be talked about in the same breath, and since few people had seen both in action, it seemed futile to make comparisons.

Arkle returned to Cheltenham for the 1966 Gold Cup, in the meantime having won the Whitbread Gold Cup, Gallaher Gold Cup, Hennessy Gold Cup and Leopardstown Chase, all carrying 12st 7lb, and the King George VI Chase. He started at 10–1 on to complete his Cheltenham hat-trick and did it by 30 lengths and more from Dormant, Snaigow and Sartorius, with the only other runner, Hunch, well behind when he fell at the third-last fence. But this was the day when Arkle came nearest to a fall.

As if to keep the public interested in what looked a lopsided contest, he all but ignored the eleventh fence, the one nearest the stands. He was already well in the lead but perhaps because he was going so easily he seemed to let his concentration slip. Whatever the reason, he ploughed through the fence in a cloud of gorse and Pat Taaffe had to show all his considerable skill as a horseman to prevent the unthinkable from happening. Arkle's quick reactions did the rest, and in a couple of strides he was back in a canter.

Arkle was to win only one more race, the SGB Handicap Chase at Ascot the following December. He was in front by the first fence and won by 15 lengths. Less than a fortnight later he returned to England for the King George VI Chase at Kempton, a race postponed for a day by bad weather. Despite making a mistake six fences from the finish, everything seemed to be moving towards another win as he took a handsome lead into the last fence, but once on the run-in he began to struggle and Dormant inched his way closer and closer and finally to the front.

The answer soon became evident. Arkle was very lame, and an X-ray revealed a fractured pedal bone in his hoof. He was treated and convalesced at the Kempton stables, where cards, presents and callers by the hundred reflected his enormous popularity. He never ran again. The National Hunt world in general, and Ireland in particular, is still searching for a successor.

Grand National Handicap Chase, 1967

Won by Foinavon – Liverpool, Saturday 8 April

They call it the world's greatest steeplechase – some call it simply the world's greatest race – and it must be more than coincidence that the winner of the first Grand National in 1839 was named Lottery. Never has the Liverpool race lived up to that name better than in 1967.

A field of 44 went to post for the race, but only one horse came back having negotiated every fence at the first time of asking. That one was Foinavon, a 100–1 shot whose owner Cyril Watkins watched the race on television at his Berkshire home and whose trainer John Kempton had a similar view at Worcester races, where he had ridden Three Dons to win a novices' hurdle. And Foinavon only got round unscathed because he was so far behind at the twenty-third fence that he missed the almighty melee that changed the whole destiny of the race.

It was a good-class turn-out, headed by the Cheltenham Gold Cup third What a Myth; the rain was a nuisance but the going

It's mayhem at the twenty-third fence as Foinavon (far right) is the only horse to clear it at his first attempt.

was perfect, and though the second favourite Bassnet fell at the first fence there was no hint of impending upset as the field set out on the second circuit. Even at Becher's for the second time most of the best-fancied horses were in contention.

At the next fence, the twenty-third and the smallest on the course, everything changed. Popham Down – an ironic name if ever there was one – had galloped round riderless after being brought down in Bassnet's fall, and at the twenty-third he made a last-second dash from the inside of the fence to the outside. First one horse and then another was brought to a halt; some ended in the bottom of the fence, some slithered helplessly over, others ground to a halt as their paths were blocked. Only one horse, Foinavon, got over safely.

Jockey John Buckingham did not realize for another three fences that he was out on his own, but he was, and that's where he stayed. Behind him, unseated jockeys frantically recovered their mounts, others turned round to take the fence again.

Foinavon and John Buckingham, in splendid isolation at the last fence.

Twenty-eight horses were caught up in the mayhem. Eight of them gave up on the spot; the other 20 took up the chase and 17 of these finished the course, but they were racing only for place money. Foinavon won by 15 lengths, while Josh Gifford on Honey End beat Brian Fletcher on Red Alligator for second place and could claim the most plausible hard-luck story of them all.

Once a stable-companion of the great Arkle, Foinavon had been sold by Anne, Duchess of Westminster, for 2,000 guineas. Cyril Watkins owned him with a friend who handed over his half-share six months before the National! John Kempton became a celebrity for a short time but soon went out of racing. John Buckingham, previously better known for riding Edward Courage's good horses and now a jockeys' valet, is still dining out on the story. As for Foinavon, who won £17,630 in stake money and £10,000 in bets for his owner that fateful afternoon, he won twice more a couple of seasons later, then earning the grand total of £461.

Prix de l'Arc de Triomphe, 1968

Won by Vaguely Noble – Longchamp, Sunday 6 October

If anyone needed confirmation that the Prix de l'Arc de Triomphe had assumed the role of Europe's most important race, the 1968 running provided it. The 17 runners included no fewer than eight individual winners of Classic races or their equivalent. There were the Derby winners of England, Ireland and Italy – Sir Ivor, Ribero and Luciano; four St Leger winners – Ribero, Samos, Dhaudevi and Luciano; the Oaks winners of England and France – La Lagune and Roseliere; and the Russian champion Zbor.

And there was Vaguely Noble, who had not won a Classic for the simple reason that he was never entered by his owner-breeder Lionel Holliday. But it was this omission which led to his turning up at Longchamp in October 1968 in the joint ownership of Robert Franklyn and Nelson Bunker Hunt and trained in France by Etienne Pollet. Sold for a world-record 136,000 guineas by the late Major Holliday's son Brook at Newmarket the previous December, Vaguely Noble had been campaigned with the sole aim of winning the Arc. It was the one achievement which would make his sale price worth the money.

Hunt, the underbidder to Franklyn at Newmarket, was urged to continue his interest and took a half-share with the eminent Hollywood plastic surgeon, in whose wife Wilma's name he ran. Part of the Hunt bargain was that the stunning two-year-old winner of two races for Newmarket trainer Walter Wharton should be transferred from Paddy Prendergast, who had taken charge of him to train in Ireland, to Pollet, where he would receive the right preparation for Longchamp.

With one exception the plan moved smoothly towards its climax. Even the setback was probably a blessing in disguise, for Vaguely Noble's unexpected defeat in the

Grand Prix de Saint-Cloud led to jockey Jean Deforge being replaced by Bill Williamson, who had ridden the colt as a two-year-old. Ice-cool Williamson was the ideal partner for the pressing engagement in the Arc.

British visitors to Longchamp who had not seen Vaguely Noble since he romped away with the Observer Gold Cup at Doncaster were in for a pleasant surprise. He had filled out into a strong and powerful colt, and his performance matched his looks. Luthier made the early running but Vaguely Noble was always handily placed, no further back than sixth, and with two furlongs to run Williamson sent him into a gap between Luthier and Roseliere. His surging gallop took him clear, and though Sir Ivor closed on him with his usual acceleration, Vaguely Noble answered every move by the Derby winner stride for relentless stride. The margin of victory was three lengths, and Vaguely Noble made it look easy.

The mission accomplished, Vaguely Noble retired to stud in the United States. Sir Ivor came out again to win the Champion Stakes and Washington DC International; his ready conqueror had nothing left to prove.

There was, however, one interesting footnote to Vaguely Noble's second season. A dispute arose over entry fees due to be paid to the Jockey Club's agents Weatherbys, which led to Mrs Franklyn's name appearing on the official black list, the Forfeit List. The money has still not been paid, and she remains unable to set foot on a British racecourse.

The moment of truth, and Vaguely Noble hits the target by beating Sir Ivor in the Prix de l'Arc de Triomphe.

Cambridgeshire Handicap, 1969

Won by Prince de Galles – Newmarket, Saturday 4 October

Preparing horses for major handicaps has long been a British tradition. Some would say it is an art; others will suggest there is more craft involved. Peter Robinson showed he had quickly picked up the knack when he won the Cambridgeshire with Prince de Galles within a few weeks of taking out a trainer's licence.

So comprehensively did Prince de Galles win one of the season's most hotly contested handicaps that this had to be among the best performances of the year, regardless of where the winner stood in the overall order of merit. He was meant to win at Newmarket; he was backed accordingly, and he did it in style.

Until September 1969 Robinson had been a jockey, making his name in major handicaps such as the Lincoln, Ebor and Royal Hunt Cup, and riding for Teddy Lambton since 1964. When financial pressures became too great for Lambton and he made a hasty exit from training, Robinson

Prince de Galles dominates the wide-open spaces of Newmarket to win the Cambridgeshire.

took over his stable, including a highly tried three-year-old called Prince de Galles.

At that advanced stage of the season Prince de Galles had had only three runs, with three months between the second and third. Two days after the Cambridgeshire weights were published, just too late to affect the big-race weights, Prince de Galles revealed his progress by finishing a close second to the 2,000 Guineas third Welsh Pageant in a Newcastle handicap. Three weeks later, over the Cambridgeshire course and distance, Prince de Galles waltzed away with a handicap by ten lengths. Victory involved no penalty for the main objective, for which Prince de Galles carried 7st 12lb, almost all of which was taken up by the very capable Frankie Durr.

Brilliantly set out for the race, and backed down to 5–2 favourite, with the rest at 100–8 and more, Prince de Galles was an incredibly easy winner of the Cambridgeshire. It was obvious after six of the nine furlongs that Durr could take the lead when he wanted, and when he did, two furlongs out, it was Prince de Galles who did what work was necessary. He won by four lengths from Grandrew; the Royal Hunt Cup winner Kamundu was a farther two lengths away third, and the rest of a 26-strong field was at least four lengths behind him.

Trainer Peter Robinson and owner Arthur Swift follow up as Frankie Durr acknowledges the cheers for Prince de Galles.

Whenever a well-backed horse wins a valuable handicap in this manner, there is a tendency either to cry 'Foul', or to blame the handicapper. Neither was the case with Prince de Galles. And proving what sort of material Robinson was working with, he started the 1970 season by being narrowly beaten in the Lincoln Handicap, and ended it by winning the Cambridgeshire again, establishing a weight-carrying record of 9st 7lb.

The Lincoln Handicap and the Goodwood Cup fell to Robinson in the next six years but his promising career ended all too prematurely in June 1978 when he was found dead in his car after suffering a heart attack while returning from the races. His son Philip has done well as a jockey in Britain and Hong Kong.

St Leger Stakes, 1970

Won by Nijinsky – Doncaster, Saturday 12 September

There's no such thing as a Triple Crown, no such trophy, no such tangible award. Yet Britain has had one since the 2,000 Guineas was first run in 1809, when it joined the Derby and St Leger as one of the three Classics open to colts. And the United States has had one since 1875, when the Kentucky Derby came along to start a Classic sequence with the Preakness Stakes and the Belmont Stakes.

The mythical treble has had 15 winners in Britain, beginning with West Australian in 1853 and ending, so far, with Nijinsky in 1970. That Nijinsky was the first to succeed since Bahram in 1935 and none has achieved it since says more about the present status of the Triple Crown itself than the ability of those eligible to take part.

Fashion has usurped tradition, for leading breeders and yearling buyers give

Nijinsky collars the Triple Crown, winning the St Leger from Meadowville and Politico (almost hidden).

The great Nijinsky is one of eight winners of the St Leger which Lester Piggott has ridden.

no points to a stallion who has won the St Leger these days. Quite the opposite; winning the oldest, longest and latest Classic of the season seems to be the kiss of death to a horse's prospects as a stallion. It is illogical, but that's fashion. Reference Point would have gone for the treble had he not missed the 2,000 Guineas through illness, but his owner-breeder belongs to the traditionalists. More to this particular point, Nashwan won the Guineas and Derby, and had the St Leger at his mercy, but his owner-breeder was not to be tempted.

Charles Engelhard and Vincent O'Brien took the bold, historical route with Nijinsky, and whatever else happened, he showed all the qualities required of a Triple Crown winner – speed to win the Guineas over a mile, adaptability to win the Derby over a mile and a half, and stamina to win the St Leger over an extended mile and three-quarters.

There were nine runners at Doncaster and Nijinsky started at 7–2 on. Rarity, another Irish runner, was second favourite, and Charlton, whom the Queen had named after the footballing brothers, third best in the betting. It was Meadowville, runner-up to Nijinsky in the Irish Sweeps Derby, who followed him home, but the margin of a length gave no indication of the winner's superiority.

A more potent reflection of Nijinsky's class was the manner in which he strode to the front fully two furlongs from the finish, leaving Lester Piggott with the task of making sure he lasted home without having a hard race. After all, the Prix de l'Arc de Triomphe was just around the corner.

Nijinsky was beaten in the Arc, and in the Champion Stakes afterwards. Excuses had to be found, and the balance of opinion – informed or otherwise – put forward the St Leger as the chief culprit. O'Brien was inclined to blame an attack of ringworm, which held up Nijinsky's work schedule in August, for giving him a hurried St Leger preparation, and he questioned whether Lester Piggott had asked Nijinsky to do too much in trying to catch Sassafras at Longchamp. But still the St Leger came out top of the hit list. After highlighting a magnificent Triple Crown winner in Nijinsky, it is a crying shame that the same race should have provided the critics with their full quota of ammunition.

Prix de l'Arc de Triomphe, 1971

Won by Mill Reef – Longchamp, Sunday 3 October

For all that Vaguely Noble achieved in 1968 in bringing the Prix de l'Arc de Triomphe to the attention of British owners, trainers and public, Mill Reef's victory in 1971 was the starting-point for a new trend. This was the race that changed the pattern for winners of the Derby and King George VI and Queen Elizabeth Stakes, and brought about a fresh approach to the autumn programme for top British-trained horses.

Apart from being beaten by Brigadier Gerard in the 2,000 Guineas, Mill Reef went through his three-year-old season undefeated. He won the Derby by two lengths from Linden Tree, the Eclipse Stakes by four lengths from Caro, and the King George VI and Queen Elizabeth Stakes by six lengths from Ortis. He was without doubt the best middle-distance horse in Europe.

As well as progressively increasing his winning margins, Mill Reef seemed to be getting better in terms of merit. The only way he could enhance his reputation was in the Prix de l'Arc de Triomphe, and that

Geoff Lewis and Mill Reef made up a partnership which might have gone on to greater things but for the colt's injury.

Once out of trouble, Mill Reef is too good for Pistol Packer.

became his objective. He did not run again between the King George at the end of July and the Arc at the beginning of October; it was a programme of summer rest followed by autumn build-up that has now become familiar.

Mill Reef's only previous excursion to France had ended in defeat, by a short head to My Swallow in the Prix Robert Papin. He had a less than comfortable journey on that occasion, but with the co-operation of the American Air Force – mindful perhaps that he was owned by the Virginian art millionaire Paul Mellon – travel was no problem this time. What traffic difficulties there were occurred through the race.

He started odds-on against 17 rivals. Some of the best of the French were missing but top local form was still well represented and the Prix Vermeille winner Pistol Packer was reckoned a powerful threat. The going was officially 'good' but it was firmer than usual at this time of year and, with a pacemaker to help the third favourite Ramsin, the early gallop was fast. It helped to establish a course record time.

Racing along the back straight and downhill towards the final turn Mill Reef was in sixth place, though the whole field was quite well bunched. That proved to be the problem, for as the pacemaker dropped back and Sharapour and Ortis went on, Mill Reef ran out of daylight on the rails. When the two leaders began to feel the pinch shortly after entering the straight and Lester Piggott dashed Hallez to the front on the outside, Mill Reef's position became slightly more worrying, though not necessarily desperate.

Geoff Lewis was alive to the potential crisis and, switching round the weakening Sharapour and Ortis, he got Mill Reef out of one hole, and nipping back inside Hallez, he escaped from another. Mill Reef did the rest, quickening away in fine style, and he ran on gamely to withstand a challenge from Pistol Packer by three lengths. Cambrizzia, who finished fastest of all from a hopeless position, took third place from Caro.

Winning the Arc meant that only Nijinsky had earned more prize-money in Europe than Mill Reef, who was the first British-trained winner of the race since Migoli in 1948, and the first British-trained Derby winner ever to win the race. He still holds the second distinction, though it can only be a matter of time before it is emulated; his stirring success was sufficient to lead others to try seriously.

Benson and Hedges Gold Cup, 1972

Won by Roberto – York, Tuesday 15 August

An easy winner, but not the one the York crowd expected as Roberto ends Brigadier Gerard's long unbeaten sequence.

Not many new races become established as quickly as the Benson and Hedges Gold Cup did. An element of the unexpected always helps, though it can rarely be planned, and this race soon built up a reputation as a graveyard for favourites, beginning with the inaugural running in 1972.

Aimed at plugging a gap in the British season at middle distances, the Benson and Hedges went straight into the European Pattern-race programme at Group 1, a rarity in itself. And the first in the series became the target for Brigadier Gerard, whose unbeaten record in 15 races stretched over two and a half seasons and included taking on the best in Europe.

It also went on the schedule for the Derby winner Roberto, who had been lifted over the line at Epsom by the powerful persuasion of Lester Piggott, only to be beaten in the Irish Sweeps Derby on his next appearance. Roberto's chance at York was so little regarded that he started at 12–1, third choice in a field of five that was headed by Brigadier Gerard at 3–1 on. Even Rheingold, narrowly beaten by Roberto in the Derby, was much preferred in the betting, after winning the Grand Prix de Saint-Cloud.

Piggott's decision to ride Rheingold instead of Roberto at York must have had some influence on the betting, especially when backers remembered that Bill Williamson had been manoeuvred off Roberto to allow Piggott the mount at Epsom. On this occasion Williamson was required to ride at Ostend, and Roberto's American owner John Galbreath turned to Braulio Baeza. That too took the British public by surprise, for Panamanian-born Baeza was unknown in this country.

In just 2 min 7.1 sec Baeza made sure everyone would know the name. That was the time, a record for York's extended mile and a quarter, it took Roberto to end Brigadier Gerard's unblemished record. And the way the race was run, there was no fluke about it. In typical American fashion Baeza shot Roberto out of the stalls to dispute the lead with the absent Mill Reef's erstwhile pacemaker Bright Beam. Baeza could not have come across a better track in Britain – dead level and left-handed – to make the most of his US experience.

Unused to such tactics, Roberto ran as if transformed. He burnt off Bright Beam before halfway and opened up a clear lead early in the straight. Rheingold was soon under pressure and Gold Rod too far behind to be a threat. Only Brigadier Gerard had a hope of catching the trail-blazer, and his star dimmed from two furlongs out. Brigadier Gerard narrowed the margin to a length but there was no stopping Roberto and as Mercer eased down on the beaten challenger, the Derby winner strode on to win by three lengths.

It was an astonishing performance, far and away Roberto's best, even allowing that he had won the Derby and was to win the Coronation Cup back at Epsom the following year. Baeza tried the same tactics in the Prix de l'Arc de Triomphe but found himself facing a familiar and similar style in Laffit Pincay, also riding for O'Brien on the St Leger winner Boucher. The two Americans took each other on at Longchamp, and Roberto finished only seventh. Though Roberto was the first three-year-old colt past the post in the Arc, Longchamp and York were worlds apart.

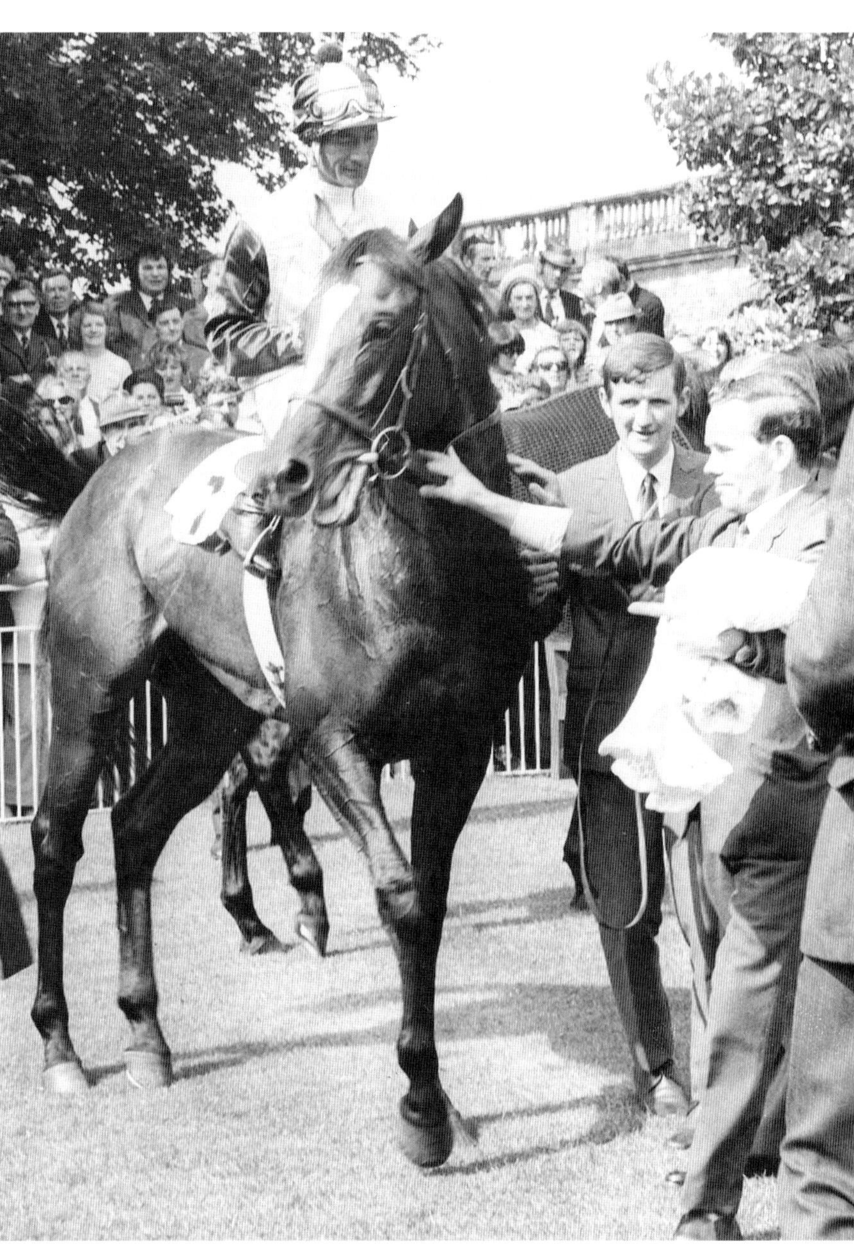

Few people knew the name Braulio Baeza before he came from the States to ride Roberto at York; everybody knew it afterwards.

Grand National Handicap Chase, 1973

Won by Red Rum – Liverpool, Saturday 31 March

Heartbreak for Crisp but joy for supporters of Red Rum, who sweeps by on the outside.

There is an exception to every rule, and the 1973 Grand National provided one to the theory that says, 'Nobody remembers a loser'. Crisp lost this race, but the public remembered his name. The fact that the winner, Red Rum, later became a folk hero is neither here nor there; he became an all-time favourite for what he did in the coming years, not for beating Crisp in 1973.

If anything, some of the shine was rubbed off Red Rum's success simply because Crisp did finish second. Crisp carried 12st to Red Rum's 10st 5lb and was beaten three-quarters of a length but it was the way he went down in defeat, rather than the facts and figures, which made the difference.

This was one of the best fields for the race for years. L'Escargot, winner of the Cheltenham Gold Cup in 1970 and 1971, shared top weight with Crisp, a star from Australia who had adapted to British conditions with remarkable ease and brilliance. Spanish Steps, winner of the 1969 Hennessy and third in the 1970 Gold Cup, was only 1lb behind them in the weights. Eighth of 38 in the handicap came Red Rum, who was rested after winning five races off the reel before the turn of the year and had shown his well-being in a steady build-up in three races on his return.

Betting on the day centred on Red Rum and Crisp, who started 9–1 joint favourites, and L'Escargot at 11–1. All three had been at longer prices when the on-course book-

It's the start of something special. Red Rum, ridden by Brian Fletcher, has won his first Grand National and is set to figure in the next four.

makers first chalked up their odds, and despite the race's reputation for providing upsets, backers were proved right.

From the start Crisp was at the centre of the action, jumping like a buck, and making nothing of the fences or their natural hazards. He was ahead by the fence after Becher's on the first circuit and had a 20-length lead passing the stands. Incredibly he seemed to step up the already hectic pace and drew even farther in front on the run down to Becher's for the second time, where Red Rum had emerged from the pack as the only runner likely to give chase.

Crisp was 20 lengths clear heading towards the third-last fence; he skipped over the second fence from home and still had a 15-length advantage at the last. Then the effort began to take its toll and jockey Richard Pitman started to become anxious. Coming to the elbow on the run-in, Crisp began to waver off the rails; he wandered like a drunken sailor suddenly meeting fresh air. Pitman picked up his whip but Crisp had nothing left; his legs carried him forward as if he were on automatic pilot. And all the time Brian Fletcher was urging Red Rum to make up the leeway. A few strides from the post Red Rum sailed past the exhausted but brave Crisp.

It might have been cruel for Crisp but it was a fairy-tale for the winner, a reject from Flat racing who had dead-heated in his first race as a two-year-old – at Liverpool, six years earlier. Bought for 6,000 guineas for Noel Le Mare, who had harboured dreams of winning the National for nearly 70 of his 80-odd years, he was trained by Donald 'Ginger' McCain at the back of his car-sales showroom in Southport and did much of his exercise on the beach.

This was the last Grand National run by the Topham family, but as one great Aintree name bowed out, another was emerging. Red Rum returned to win the 1974 National under 12st; he was second in 1975 and 1976; and won again in 1977. He was due to turn out for a sixth time in 1978 but was injured shortly before the race and was retired. Already famous for his unprecedented National exploits, he has become even more renowned for his public appearances.

Prix de l'Arc de Triomphe, 1974

Won by Allez France – Longchamp, Sunday 6 October

Allez France, a beautiful filly, and Yves Saint-Martin, perhaps France's best-ever jockey.

A poor draw and a less-than-fit jockey could not prevent Allez France from gaining her finest hour, but how the adoring French crowd would have reacted had the winning margin of a head gone the other way is easy to imagine. Reputations count for nothing in France if a well-fancied horse is beaten, and Allez France, as well as being a huge favourite with the general public, was favourite for the Arc.

It was her second outing in the race; 12 months previously she failed to match only the might of Rheingold and Lester Piggott. By coincidence Piggott had been signed up to ride Allez France this year, after her regular jockey Yves Saint-Martin seemed to be losing a battle for fitness.

Saint-Martin, who formed a perfect combination with Allez France – which had already won four races at Longchamp that season – was thrown in the paddock at Maisons-Laffitte ten days before the Arc. He broke a small bone high in his thigh and was told by the doctor he would be out for three weeks. Presumably the doctor did not immediately appreciate the urgent need for recovery!

But Saint-Martin set himself a stiff get-fit regime, and, armed with a pain-killer and bound by a corset, he declared himself able to ride. Maybe the thought of surrendering to the man who beat him the previous year was a spur.

Allez France was drawn towards the outside of the high-class field of 20 runners, which on the one hand helped Saint-Martin adopt his usual waiting tactics but on the other pushed him farther behind than he wanted. After two furlongs, Allez France had five behind her; making the final turn four furlongs from the finish, she still had 14 in front. But she accelerated so quickly early in the straight that she opened up a commanding lead in a matter of strides. She had hit the front far too soon, Saint-Martin said. But her class and courage carried her through, and though Comtesse de Loir put in a strong run, and at one stage looked like winning, the runner-up was being held at bay in the last few strides.

'I was relieved and happy': that was how Saint-Martin summed up his feelings a few years later. He probably still gets a shiver down his neck when he thinks how close he came to being beaten on the Queen of Longchamp. Yet the instant speed shown by Allez France when she took off into the lead marked her out as a truly fine filly. Saint-Martin decided there was no point in holding her back, and she had enough left in the tank to beat the strongest set of runners in a European middle-distance race all season.

Allez France returned for her third Arc the following year at the age of five. She went into the race the best middle-distance older horse in Europe, having won three of her four races, all at Longchamp. She came out of it no longer quite the best, finishing fifth to the German-trained long-shot Star Appeal. She was beaten more than eight lengths, but would probably have been much closer had she not suffered interference around the halfway mark. She came back with a cut hind leg and one of her shoes torn off. Though nothing had ruffled her previously, she ran without much enthusiasm in two races after the Arc and was retired. She owed no one a penny.

The crowning moment for Allez France, who wins the Prix de l'Arc de Triomphe from Comtesse de Loir and Margouillat.

King George VI and Queen Elizabeth Diamond Stakes, 1975

Won by Grundy – Ascot, Saturday 26 July

Starting to compile a list of great horse races is easy; it only gets harder after nominating the duel between Grundy and Bustino at Ascot, where the wordsmiths ran out of superlatives.

'Not since the great battle between Quashed and America's Omaha in the 1936 Gold Cup have we seen a better race on Ascot's Royal Heath,' The *Sporting Life*'s Len Thomas wrote. 'It was a pity that one of them had to be beaten.'

'The highlight of the racing year, a race to remember,' was how *Racehorses of 1975* described it, adding that it was 'a finish that must have resembled that famous finish between Ard Patrick and Sceptre in the Eclipse of long ago that George Lambton remembered and described with ease and pleasure'.

Keeping strictly to the moment, the *Observer*'s Hugh McIlvanney wrote: 'Only those with iced water for blood could remain aloof from the excitement that flooded through the stands at Ascot ... a struggle of ferocious, unyielding intensity over the last two furlongs ... a glittering, flawless example of horseracing at its most irresistible.'

It was Dick Hern, trainer of the four-year-old Bustino, who set up the race. He knew the year-younger Grundy, winner of the Irish 2,000 Guineas, Derby and Irish Sweeps Derby, had more speed than his colt. If Bustino were to win Britain's premier middle-distance race, with its £82,000 first prize backed by the diamond firm De Beers, the favourite's cutting edge had to be blunted.

To achieve that would require a fast, even pace from the start, and no one horse in Hern's stable was capable of setting the conditions once Bustino's regular pacesetter Riboson had been ruled out through injury. Hern solved the matter by running two pacemakers, the miler Highest and the stayer Kinglet.

Highest, ridden by Frankie Durr, led for the first four and a half furlongs, then Kinglet, ridden by Eric Eldin, took over for almost a mile. All the while Joe Mercer had Bustino handily placed in third or fourth position as his stablemates hurtled along at full pelt. As Kinglet began to feel the strain, Bustino was sent to the front before reaching Ascot's shortish final straight of two and a half furlongs. Mercer's ploy took Bustino four lengths clear, as Grundy struggled for a moment to keep in touch, but Pat Eddery, fully alive to the tactics, still had Grundy in second place as they turned for home.

From that point it was a two-horse race;

Grundy edges out Bustino in what has become known as the Race of the Century.

the rest of a high-class field didn't have a prayer. Bustino galloped on strongly, but Grundy was catching him on the outside and he poked his bright chestnut nose in front with a furlong to run. Bustino would not give in and battled back under Mercer's rhythmic driving, but Grundy was just the stronger for Eddery's powerful persuasion and as Bustino's tongue rolled out, the prize was won.

The margin of victory was half a length and the time, inevitably, a mile-and-a-half course record of 2min 26.98sec, almost two and a half seconds faster than the previous best. Beating the clock did not automatically mean these were super-horses; if the conditions are right, average horses will set time records. But these two *were* outstanding, and they finished at least five lengths in front of a field headed by Dahlia, winner of the race for the previous two years.

Bustino never ran again; Grundy ran once more and was well beaten behind Dahlia in the Benson and Hedges Gold Cup. The heroes had had their day at Ascot.

Joe Coral Eclipse Stakes, 1976

Won by Wollow – Sandown Park, Saturday 3 July

Doping is an emotive subject in any sport, but particularly so in horseracing, where in Britain it is usually allied to betting interests. The nature of the business is that doping to win is associated with trying to put one over the bookmakers, while doping to lose is regarded as the bookmaker's way of tilting the balance his way. Bookmakers fume at the suggestion that they are always the prime suspects, but that is the way of public perception.

Britain's rules about doping have always been tough; once a positive test was discovered the horse had to be disqualified and the trainer punished. At one time the trainer was also automatically disqualified, but that rigid penalty was subsequently relaxed, though he still remains ultimately responsible for any breach of the rule.

Administering drugs to bring a horse to peak performance, and keep him there, is slightly different from giving him a prohibited substance for a specific occasion and purpose, but Britain still maintains a closed mind and a stiff testing procedure. The impression was that other countries might not be quite so vigilant, so when the French began to carry all before them in Britain in 1976, rumours inevitably began to circulate.

They remained rumours as Flying Water won the 1,000 Guineas, Empery the Derby, Pawneese the Oaks, Sagaro the Gold Cup at

The race goes fine, as Trepan wins comfortably from Wollow, but then the trouble started.

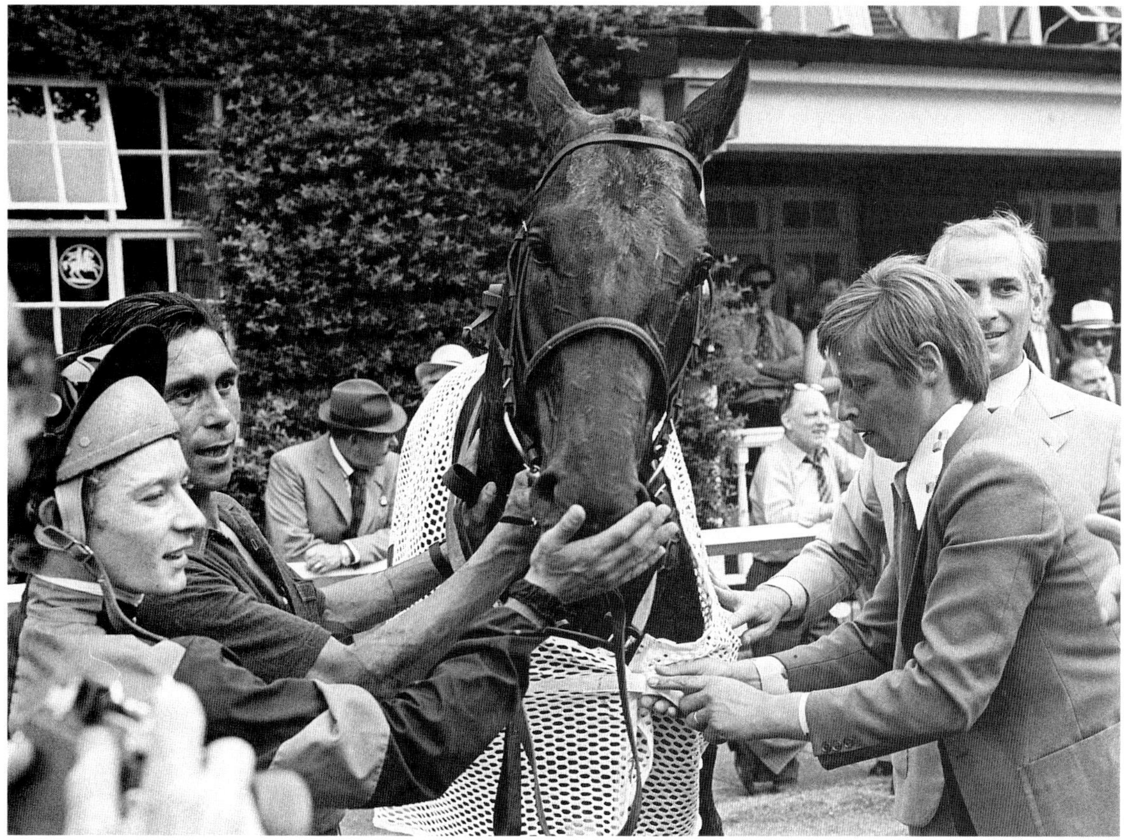

No cause for concern as Trepan cools off in the Sandown Park winner's enclosure. Almost five months later he was disqualified.

Royal Ascot, and Trepan the Prince of Wales's Stakes and the Eclipse Stakes. Then came the bombshell; Trepan's routine dope tests after his wins at Royal Ascot and Sandown had proved positive.

Both Trepan's victories had been stunning. He went to Royal Ascot after winning a handicap at Longchamp and swept past Anne's Pretender to win by two and a half lengths in record time. Less than three weeks later he returned for the Group 1 Eclipse and trounced the 2,000 Guineas winner Wollow by two lengths, also beating the course record. Here, it seemed, was a top-class horse who had appeared almost from nowhere. Little wonder that some smug smiles were seen around the racecourses when the Jockey Club revealed the results of the post-race tests.

The Jockey Club's disciplinary stewards dealt with both cases at an inquiry on 12 August, almost five weeks after Sandown, and it was inevitable that Trepan would be disqualified, costing his owner £49,585 in first-prize-money. Trainer François Boutin was fined a total of £1,250 – £500 each for two breaches of the rules at Royal Ascot, and £250 for one at Sandown – and a stable lad was fined £100 for the Ascot affair.

But was this doping of the nefarious kind? The Jockey Club took the view that it was more a technicality, for they could have disqualified Boutin and asked the French authorities to do likewise.

Boutin told the inquiry that traces of caffeine and theobromine found in the urine sample taken after Royal Ascot had come from a diuretic given by mistake to Trepan the day before the race; normally the 'cleaning-out' treatment was stopped three days ahead of racing. The Jockey Club accepted his explanation, and by their leniency over Sandown seemed to suggest that traces of theobromine, which were found after Sandown, could have remained in the horse's system between the two races.

Trepan came back to England for the Benson and Hedges Gold Cup at York five days after the Jockey Club inquiry. He finished last of seven as Wollow beat another French runner, Crow. Trepan finished fourth of seven in his next race, in France, and thirteenth of 20 in the Prix de l'Arc de Triomphe. No one knew quite what to make of him, but Boutin's reputation was totally untarnished by the incidents.

GOLD CUP, 1977

Won by Sagaro – Royal Ascot, Thursday 16 June

Stayers have become an endangered species in European racing. Ever since the Aga Khan, the leading breeder in the immediate post-War years, described the three most desirable attributes of a racehorse as speed, speed and more speed, the writing had been on the wall. Horses best suited to long distances have steadily fallen victim to fashion.

Yet as long as variety remains the spice of British racing life, a genuinely top-class stayer with a turn of foot will emerge now and then. Even though commercial breeders may avoid him like the plague, traditionalists will take him to their hearts. Sagaro is the best example of the last 25 years. More than that, he is probably the best winner of the Gold Cup at Royal Ascot in the last 40 years.

Sagaro wins his third Gold Cup at Ascot, where he and Lester Piggott were unbeatable. In a clean sweep for French-trained horses he beat Buckskin (left), Citoyen and the first English horse, the grey Bruni.

Sceptics may argue that the competition to Sagaro was not what it might have been. After all, they will say, Classic winners don't go on to race in the Gold Cup these days and the best horses are campaigned at around a mile and a half. 'What is the merit in winning over two and a half miles?' they will ask.

That's all very well, but Sagaro could do no more than beat with ease those who did take him on, and his form was not far short of the very best. He should not be denigrated simply because he could not match strides with middle-distance horses.

In his own sphere Sagaro was an outstanding champion, who became the first horse since the Gold Cup was instituted in 1807 to win the race three times. The shame was that his financial rewards came nowhere near what he would have earned in races of similar status at shorter distances. For winning three Gold Cups, Sagaro collected a little over £56,000. In 1977 the Derby was worth £107,530 to the winner, and the King George VI and Queen Elizabeth Diamond Stakes £88,355.

Bred and owned by the Swiss-based financier Gerry Oldham and trained by François Boutin in France, Sagaro was ridden in England by Lester Piggott, who has had no peers in the Gold Cup. When Sagaro completed his hat-trick, Piggott was riding his eighth winner of the race, and he has since won three more, one on Le Moss and two on Ardross.

When Sagaro first came to Ascot, in 1975, he turned the tables on Le Bavard, who had beaten him in France's equivalent to the Gold Cup, the Prix du Cadran. He won by four lengths but the margin could have been doubled had Piggott seen fit to apply maximum force. The following year Sagaro easily won the Prix du Cadran and was equally impressive at Ascot, where his turn of speed took him to the front below the distance and he won cosily by a length.

In 1977 Sagaro was again unsuccessful in the Prix du Cadran, going down by three-quarters of a length to Buckskin, who had pulled off the remarkable feat of beating Sagaro three times in a row, though each time by a diminishing margin. This was enough to cause Buckskin to start favourite at Ascot, but with Piggott – who had not ridden Sagaro since the same race a year previously – back in the saddle this was where the run ended.

Yves Saint-Martin made the running on Buckskin and led into the straight from Sagaro and the 1975 St Leger winner Bruni, who soon dropped back. The two favourites came clear, with Piggott easing towards the centre of the course to make his challenge. Sagaro quickened a furlong out and that was that. He swept five lengths clear and a third Gold Cup was won as impressively as the first two.

Sagaro did not run again. He was bought by the National Stud for £175,000, peanuts compared to what a horse of his class would have been worth as a middle-distance winner.

IRISH SWEEPS DERBY, 1978

Won by Shirley Heights – The Curragh, Saturday 1 July

Shirley Heights was an old-fashioned type of horse, bred by his owner and designed to stay every yard of the Classic distance of a mile and a half. It was good to see him emerge through his three-year-old season, even though injury forced him into retirement earlier than anticipated.

Owner-breeders have declined in number and influence over the last 25 years, and horses bred specifically to be at their best over 12 furlongs, rather than ten, have got thinner on the ground. Lord Halifax, and later his son, did his best to keep pace, and Shirley Heights did credit to his ambitions.

The last race in which Shirley Heights ran, the Irish Sweeps Derby, was well into its second phase of tradition. Previously largely overlooked by British owners, except as a consolation prize occasionally targeted for Epsom also-rans, the Irish Derby took on a fresh complexion when the Irish Hospitals Sweepstake, the most famous lottery in the world, began lending support in 1962.

In 1961 the winner of the Irish Derby earned £7,921; in 1962 the value of the race was more than £67,000 and the winner, Tambourine II, picked up £50,277 for his owner Mrs Howell Jackson. Total prize-money for the first Irish Hospital Sweepstake on the race was £3.25 million and 26 people each won first prizes of £50,000. The odds were slightly tilted in favour of Mrs Jackson, though she had to pay more for her ticket!

With this sort of encouragement the Irish Sweeps Derby, as it was now called, became an instant hit with owners, and the Derby winner had a ready-made target after Epsom. Shirley Heights became the fifth horse to complete the double, following Santa Claus, Nijinsky, Grundy and The Minstrel. Five more have since emulated Shirley Heights – Troy, Shergar, Shahrastani, Kahyasi and Generous.

At Epsom, Shirley Heights had had to bring all his stamina into play to pip

Hawaiian Sound in the last few strides. Bill Shoemaker, riding in England for the first time, seemed anxious to get back to the States as quickly as possible as he set a hectic pace on Hawaiian Sound, which had broken most of his rivals by the time they straightened for home. Shirley Heights had lost ground down Tattenham Hill and had ten in front of him with a little over three furlongs to run. Greville Starkey sent him about his business and, making for the rails as Shoemaker allowed Hawaiian Sound to drift to his right, he drove Shirley Heights in front to snatch victory by a head. It was a first Derby win for Starkey and trainer John Dunlop.

At The Curragh, Shirley Heights won by the same margin, but this time Exdirectory was second, with Shoemaker and Hawaiian Sound a neck down in third place. The finish was as furious as the margins suggested, and again stamina was Shirley Heights' trump card as he was made to work even harder than at Epsom.

Hawaiian Sound went off in front, going at a good lick, but was headed at halfway. Shirley Heights was already flat to the boards when Hawaiian Sound regained the lead two furlongs out, but he answered Starkey's every call, closely pursued by Exdirectory. The challengers came wide of Hawaiian Sound, who was caught in the dying stages of a Derby for the second time. Here, though, two touched him off, with Shirley Heights just the stronger.

It was planned to run Shirley Heights in the St Leger, where the distance was tailor-made for him, but shortly before he was due to reappear at York in August he was injured. He retired to the National Stud and has done extremely well, siring the Derby winner Slip Anchor and the French Derby winner Darshaan.

In a gruelling race across the broad sweep of The Curragh, Shirley Heights is too good for Exdirectory and Hawaiian Sound.

Tote-Ebor Handicap, 1979

Won by Sea Pigeon – York, Wednesday 22 August

A jump jockey wins one of the most competitive handicaps on the Flat: it could only happen in Britain or Ireland. And it happened here, in Britain, with an Irishman in the saddle.

Sea Pigeon was bred to win a Derby, and after his American breeder John Hay Whitney sent him to England to be trained by Jeremy Tree, he did run at Epsom, finishing seventh to Morston. But he disappointed in two later races, was gelded and early the next year was sold for about £10,000 to the Scottish owner Pat Muldoon. So began one of the fairy-tales of recent times as Sea Pigeon went into training first with Gordon Richards in Cumbria and then with Peter Easterby in Yorkshire.

A slice of luck for Sea Pigeon, who dodges Golden Cygnet to win the Scottish Champion Hurdle.

By the time the nine-year-old Sea Pigeon reached York for the Ebor Handicap he had become a star under both codes. He won the Ladbroke Chester Cup and Vaux Breweries Gold Tankard in both 1977 and 1978, as well as the amateur riders' Derby, the Moet & Chandon Silver Magnum, in 1978. He had also started to move up the ladder in the hurdling world, winning the Scottish Champion Hurdle twice and finishing fourth, second and second in the real thing at Cheltenham.

Not many horses combine the two disciplines of Flat and hurdles racing as Sea Pigeon did; they usually start in one and progress to the other. But he kept going at both, to such purpose that his efforts took him to the top of the weights for the Ebor. Carrying 10st, he was rated 9lb above the next horse, Arapahos, who had finished third in the Gold Cup at Royal Ascot. Trainer Easterby had another runner, No Bombs, who was set to carry 8st 7lb.

Mark Birch, Easterby's stable jockey, was Sea Pigeon's rider on the 21 occasions he had raced outside amateurs' events since he moved north, but he could ride at 8st 7lb without carrying dead weight in the saddle and so he went on No Bombs. The ride on Sea Pigeon was handed to Jonjo O'Neill, his regular hurdles jockey, who had done very

Jonjo O'Neill is almost caught napping on Sea Pigeon as Donegal Prince (rails) fights back.

little Flat racing since his days as an apprentice in Ireland. In the event, he was lucky to be allowed to ride, but probably more fortunate not to lose future rides altogether.

O'Neill paced the race under Sea-Pigeon's big weight, beginning to improve soon after the turn for home about three furlongs from the finish. They continued to make progress all the way up the straight and headed the leader Donegal Prince approaching the final furlong. The race was won, but it wasn't over.

With an unusual burst of over-confidence O'Neill eased off and dropped his hands on to Sea Pigeon's neck. That was the signal for the old horse to relax, but as he did so Donegal Prince, on whom Philip Robinson had never given up working, fought back. They went past the post stride for stride; O'Neill thought – hoped – he had won, but trainer Easterby reckoned he had been beaten. The judge consulted the photo-finish print and declared Sea Pigeon the winner by a short head. If he had been operating in more accurate measurement, he would have said it was two inches, or three at the most.

Had Sea Pigeon lost the Ebor the repercussions for O'Neill might have been devastating. Instead, he continued the partnership until injury intervened. He rode Sea Pigeon six more times on the Flat, and won three, including a third Vaux Breweries Gold Tankard. He rode him for one more season over hurdles and won three out of six races, including the Champion Hurdle. O'Neill was injured when Sea Pigeon won his second Champion in 1981.

However, only a little bit of blarney enabled O'Neill to partner Sea Pigeon in the Ebor at all. A week before the race he was riding at Dundalk and struck his foot against the running rail, breaking three toes. The regulations said he had to pass the doctor at York before he could ride again, and it was with some trepidation that he faced an examination of his foot. The doctor manipulated the toes and pronounced him fit to ride. He might have ruled differently if he had examined the foot with the broken toes.

2,000 Guineas Stakes, 1980

Won by Known Fact – Newmarket, Saturday 3 May

Since racehorses do not run on tram lines, and are strong enough to ignore their riders' instructions on a whim, interference is always a danger. It's the degree of interference, its causes and its effects that provoke most arguments. And no Jockey Club rule is more debated than this one.

The 1980 2,000 Guineas prompted more discussion than in most instances, because the best horse in the race was eventually placed last. That the horse in question, Nureyev, also started a well-backed favourite only fanned the flames of controversy.

It was inevitable that Nureyev would lose his place, for he seriously hampered Posse about two furlongs from the finish. The question was where he would be placed. As the rules stood, he would automatically be placed last if the stewards decided his jockey had been guilty of 'dangerous, reckless, careless or improper' riding. If they felt the interference had been caused accidentally, they had to decide whether the result had been affected, after which they could confirm the placings or put Nureyev behind the horse he hampered.

There was hardly any doubt about the nature of the interference; jockey Philippe Paquet had not been involved in an accident. Indeed, one commentator reckoned he would have been equally at home in the Rugby League cup final which took place that day.

Paquet seemed so overwhelmingly confident about the outcome that he set Nureyev a ridiculously hard task, settling last of the 14-strong line-up, at least ten lengths behind the leaders until halfway. There, he began to pick up ground, but the race was beginning in earnest and all routes to the front had been blocked off. There was hardly enough time to pull back and come round the outside, so Paquet decided on the only option he could think of, and barged his way through.

Nureyev quickened in the style of a useful horse and got up to beat Known Fact, who had enjoyed a troublefree passage along the rails, by a neck. Less than a length behind in third place came the unfortunate Posse, who had almost been brought down as Nureyev quickstepped through. The best horse in the race had passed the post first, but Posse had been beaten by less than the distance he forfeited in the incident.

Under the rules operating at that time, Nureyev could expect to be placed third, if the stewards deemed the interference accidental, or last, if they took a stricter line. After a 50-minute inquiry, they found Paquet guilty of reckless riding, and for the fifth time in a British Classic a 'winner' was placed last.

Nureyev and his connections lost £56,620 in first-prize-money; his backers lost everything. And those critics who believe the horse and jockey should be separated in these cases – as is done in Australia – had a field day.

Their argument is that where a horse deserves to earn prize-money but a jockey deserves to be punished for a misdemeanour, both conditions can be satisfied. In this instance, they say, Nureyev should have

been demoted to third, behind Posse, but Paquet should have been punished according to his undisputed crime.

The Jockey Club takes the view that owner, trainer, rider and horse must be considered as a team, and not as separate individuals. It thought at this time, and still does, that the 'win-at-all-costs' idea was not one it wanted to promote. A jockey must not be tempted to throw caution to the winds, safe in the knowledge that though he may be punished, prize-money and bets would be collected and he would stand to be recompensed.

Following frequent discussion the rules on interference were altered at the end of the 1980s, so that in cases of accidental interference the stewards have discretion to confirm the placings if the horse causing an incident did not improve its position as a result. It is a subtle but important difference. But anything other than accidental interference incurs automatic disqualification. Nureyev would still have lost the 2,000 Guineas, but he would not have lost everything.

A picture of the one that got away. Nureyev faces the cameras; soon his connections were facing the fact they had lost the 2,000 Guineas on a disqualification.

Sun Grand National Handicap Chase, 1981

Won by Aldaniti – Liverpool, Saturday 4 April

Every Grand National has a hero; in 1981 there were two, Aldaniti and Bob Champion. They would have made the main sports news simply for winning the race. That each had triumphed over terrible adversity in getting to Liverpool pushed them on to the front pages and to the head of the television and radio bulletins.

Aldaniti had run only once in 16 months before he went to Liverpool, and Champion had had barely a handful of rides since he resumed after conquering cancer. In the build-up to the race they attracted more than sympathetic curiosity, for Aldaniti had a serious chance of winning. After the race they were talked about for months; a feature film was even made about them. Theirs was a heartening story in the best traditions of the British romantic novel, except that their story was real.

Champion was told he had cancer in July 1979, a few months before Aldaniti finished badly lame in a race at Sandown. It was the third time Aldaniti had broken down and his future was uncertain. Champion's appeared worse, for he was warned he might only have months to live.

It was almost a year before Champion

Aldaniti makes little of the last fence (left), after showing his style at the twenty-seventh (right), and the dream result is about to become reality.

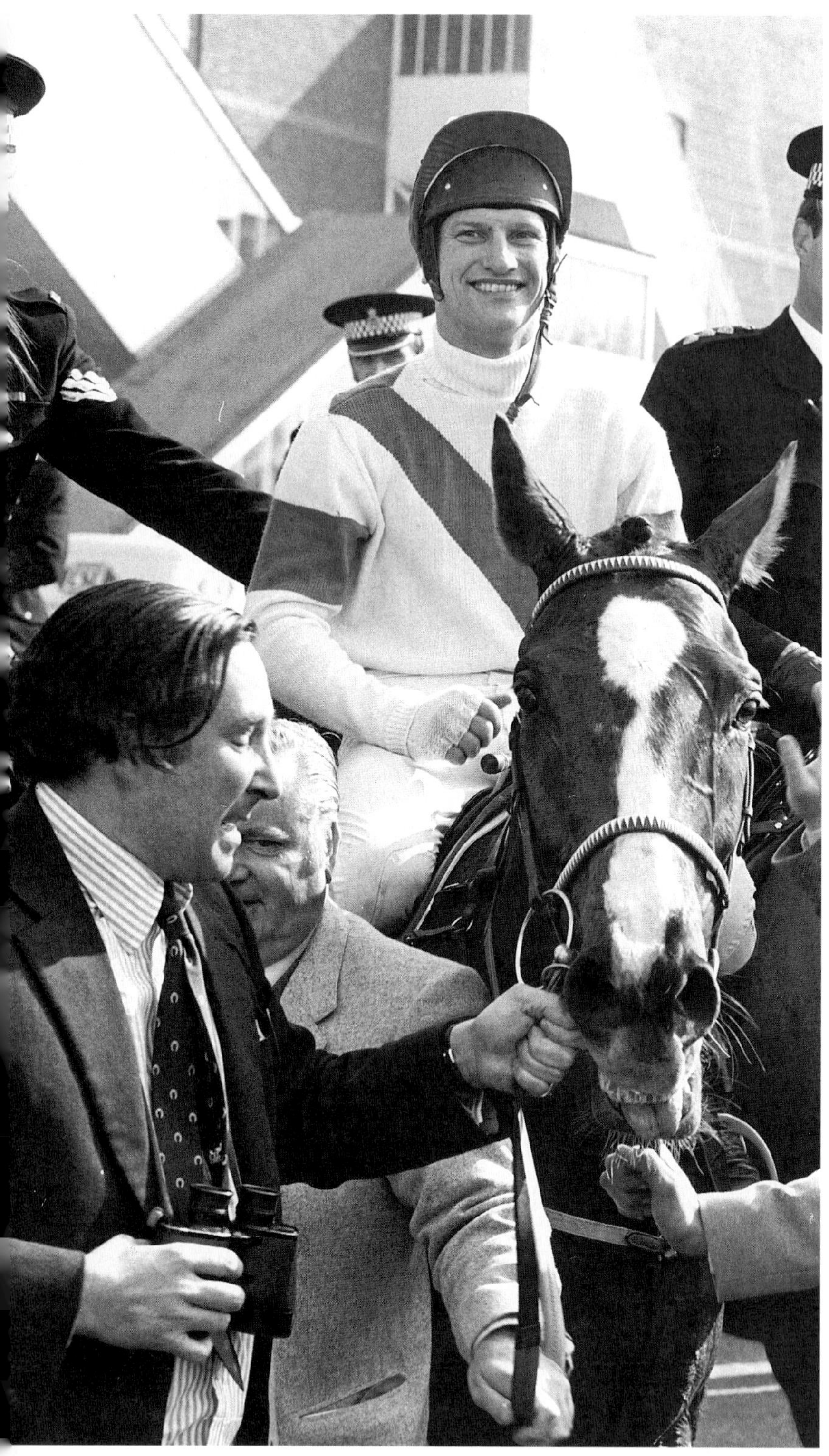

Even Aldaniti seems to be smiling as he and Bob Champion are greeted by owner Nick Embiricos.

acknowledged his illness in public, during which time he went through the agonies of six demanding courses of chemotherapy treatment. He admitted later that the thought of being fit and well enough to ride Aldaniti in the Grand National had driven him on.

In the spring of 1980, when he was allowed to leave hospital, Champion was ready to begin the slow process of regaining his strength and fitness. He sought the warmth of South Carolina and at the end of May, in Maryland, he rode in a race for the first time since the onset of illness. It was on the Flat, and he won. By the time he returned to England his fight for life was public knowledge, and he had his first ride back in this country at the end of August. Within a month he won for the first time, on Physicist, trained like Aldaniti by Josh Gifford.

Gradually Champion grew stronger but race-riding was still hard work and trainers seemed wary of whether he could cope. Gifford supported him, and Aldaniti gave him strength, for in December he returned to training. They were reunited at Ascot in February, and despite being off the track for so long, Aldaniti seemed as good as new. He won a competitive handicap by four lengths, and the Grand National became more than a dream.

Aldaniti carried 10st 13lb at Liverpool and started second favourite to Spartan Missile, whose owner-breeder-trainer, 54-year-old John Thorne, was also his rider. They finished first and second, so whichever had won there would have been a story. That it was Aldaniti who came to the famous winning post in front was incredible.

Having pitched on his nose at the first fence, Aldaniti dropped towards the rear of the field but, racing on the inside, he pulled his way to the front after the eleventh fence – only 19 to go. Three other runners kept him company for a few fences but he was definitely in front again at the seventeenth, and crossing the Melling Road, two fences from home, he and Royal Mail were clear.

Royal Mail blundered away his winning chance at the second-last fence and was headed by the fast-improving Spartan Missile halfway up the long run-in. Champion and Aldaniti had come too far to be beaten now, and though Spartan Missile continued to close the gap beyond where the course bends round an elbow, he had nothing left to offer in the last 50 yards and Aldaniti rallied to win by four lengths.

Tears came easily at Liverpool that day.

William Hill Stewards' Cup Handicap, 1982

Won by Soba – Goodwood, Tuesday 27 July

David Nicholls brings Soba wide of the field to head the cavalry charge at Goodwood.

When the Jockey Club introduced centralized handicapping in the 1970s, and its officials were given responsibility for separate distance categories rather than individual race meetings, trainers grumbled that part of the art of their job was being taken away. Instead of being able to pick and choose their races, exploiting opportunities where they felt the handicapper had underestimated their horses, they had to work around a universal assessment. They reckoned without David Chapman.

When one of Chapman's horses begins to improve, there's no telling where it will finish. In 1982 his three-year-old filly Soba ended by winning 11 of her 14 races and running second in two others. Six of her wins were in handicaps, and on the only occasion she was farther back than second place she finished slightly lame.

Chapman's name, and that of his jockey David Nicholls, probably meant nothing to most racegoers at Goodwood on Stewards' Cup day. They rarely ventured farther south than Doncaster, and there were no obvious stars in Chapman's stables at Stillington on the outskirts of York. Soba might have been a little more familiar, for her form figures for the season read: six wins and a nowhere.

Soba was at her best when she could set off in front and stay there. The tactics paid off handsomely in the Stewards' Cup.

Her unplaced run in a sponsored handicap at Ayr brought to an end a winning sequence that began in a maiden event at Thirsk in May, when she started at 33–1, and ran quickly through races at Hamilton, Catterick (twice) and Thirsk. After Ayr, Chapman had 17 days to get her over the effects of a trapped nerve in her off-hind leg, and he enlisted the aid of Janet Ellis, a physiotherapist from Harrogate. Their combined skill got her safely to Goodwood, and Soba's quicksilver speed did the rest.

There were plenty of experts who ruled out her chance because she was drawn closest to the stands rails; the general view was that in a maximum field of 30 over the lightning-fast six-furlong course it was best to be drawn nearer the far side, where most of the runners would race. But the Stewards' Cup has been won by horses from the lowest draw in recent years. Arcandy came from there in 1957, as did Jukebox when he beat the horse drawn next to him in 1970. Both had made most of the running, and that was Soba's style.

Nicholls bounced her out of the starting stalls in a flash and after a furlong she held a definite advantage. The farther she went, the less likely it was that she would be caught, and though her jockey never relaxed, she won unchallenged by two and a half lengths. The draw made no difference, but her blistering speed from the start did.

Soba carried on the good work after Goodwood and eventually earned her chance of taking on some of the best sprinters in the country. What's more, Chapman is not the sort of trainer to let a horse in form rest on its laurels, and more than once she had two races within a few days of each other. Soba showed no ill effects, and when she faced her biggest test, in the Diadem Stakes at Ascot, she ran right up to her best. It was not quite good enough to beat Indian King but she did not go down without her customary fight.

Soba raced for one more season, and though she was not so successful in numbers of wins – two from ten races – she showed even better form, tackling the best all season, and won the same amount of total prize-money, around £82,000, as she had the previous year. Considering she cost Chapman and his sister the grand total of £728 to produce – £350 for her sire's services and 360 guineas to buy her dam – she more than paid her way, and gave a lot of people an enormous amount of pleasure into the bargain.

Tote Cheltenham Gold Cup, 1983

Won by Bregawn – Thursday 17 March

It was odds-on that Michael Dickinson would win this year's Cheltenham Gold Cup. After all, he trained five of the 11 runners and they were in the first eight in the betting. As for his team finishing first, second, third, fourth and fifth, that was a different matter. But it happened.

Dickinson's training career over jumps lasted four seasons, but before he left to join Robert Sangster in an ill-fated venture at Manton which lasted one Flat season, his short spell in succession to his father Tony was spectacularly successful. It was marked by his exhaustive attention to detail and consuming passion for innovation. If he heard about a new schedule for training athletes, he wanted to know if it would work for horses. If he came across someone with a new idea, he would question them intently.

It was his interest in statistics and detail which led to his attack on the world-record number of winners in a day. He took pains to discover what the existing record was, and set out to beat it on 27 December 1982, an ideal day because of the plethora of meetings. His 21 runners set off for six courses, and returned to his stables at Harewood in West Yorkshire with 12 first prizes, beating the record of ten set in Australia by Colin Hayes.

Saddling five runners in the Cheltenham Gold Cup was slightly different, though no less a challenge for Dickinson, who rightly reckoned it was an achievement to have five

In a sea of faces Graham Bradley's delight stands out as he returns on Bregawn.

Michael Dickinson and the Famous Five – (from the left) Ashley House, Captain John, Bregawn, Wayward Lad and Silver Buck.

fit horses good enough to take to the season's premier steeplechase. Once they arrived there, they would try their best, wherever they finished.

In 1982 he sent out Silver Buck and Bregawn to finish first and second in the race. A year later they were back, joined by Captain John, Wayward Lad and Ashley House. Finding jockeys for the five was easy. Graham Bradley, Robert Earnshaw and amateur Dermot Browne were attached to the stable; they rode Bregawn, Silver Buck and Ashley House respectively. Jonjo O'Neill had no mount following the retirement of Night Nurse on New Year's Day, and rode Wayward Lad. David Goulding, a more-than-capable northern jockey, had won on Captain John the previous year when he was trained elsewhere.

Each of Dickinson's runners had won on his previous appearance – Bregawn at Hereford and Silver Buck at Market Rasen when no starting prices were returned; Captain John at odds-on in an amateurs' handicap chase at Kelso; Wayward Lad in the King George VI Chase as one of the December dozen; and Ashley House at odds-on in a conditions chase at Doncaster. Choosing his races carefully was Dickinson's trademark.

Other stables were represented at Cheltenham – notably Fred Winter with Fifty Dollars More and Brown Chamberlin, and David Elsworth with Combs Ditch – but as the leaders made their way down the hill to the second-last fence, history was already in the making. Bregawn, who had gone to the front at the fifth fence, was leading from Wayward Lad, with Silver Buck and Captain John chasing, and Ashley House battling gallantly to stay with his stablemates. The rest had either fallen, been pulled up or given up the ghost.

Bregawn drew away up the final hill and won by five lengths from Captain John, who jumped the last fence almost upsides the leader, with Wayward Lad a length and a half away third. Silver Buck was beaten a distance into fourth, and 25 lengths farther behind came Ashley House.

For the first time, five horses were allowed into a winner's enclosure built to accommodate four. It's most unlikely that Cheltenham, or any other course for that matter, will have occasion to bend this rule again.

Dinsdale Spa Stakes, 1984

Won by Provideo – Redcar, Thursday 1 November

A race worth £1,452 to the winner, run at Redcar in North Yorkshire at 3.30 on a Thursday afternoon in November, when the favourite started at 8–1 on, would normally attract scant attention beyond those taking part. This was different, for the progress of the odds-on Provideo had been followed with increasing interest.

Provideo was a normal horse in most respects, but not all. This was his twenty-third race of the season, and winning it enabled him to equal a record which had stood for 99 years. It was Provideo's sixteenth win. He was already the most successful two-year-old of the century; now he joined The Bard with the highest number of victories ever recorded by a horse of that age.

It was a prodigious feat, which heaped enormous credit on trainer Bill O'Gorman and his staff at Newmarket, jockey Tony Ives and Provideo himself. And it earned Provideo the title Horse of the Year in the Racegoers' Club's poll of racing journalists, the only time the award has gone either to a two-year-old or a horse who was not a champion in his or her category.

Provideo did win a race at Ripon called the Champion Two Years Old Trophy, but the name owes more to the hopes and aspirations of the racecourse than the quality of runners. At the end of the season the Jockey Club handicapper rated Provideo at 8st 9lb in the Free Handicap; he was 12lb

Provideo is on his way to a twentieth-century record, winning at Sandown Park.

Tony Ives and Provideo equalled a record which had stood for 99 years.

behind the top weight Kala Dancer, and there were 44 horses between them. But none of those above him in the rankings could lay claim to half his work-rate.

Like The Bard all those years before him, Provideo started his career at the first meeting of the season in the Brocklesby Stakes. There, except in numbers of wins, the similarity ends. The Bard, who was never beaten as a two-year-old, had no opposition in one 'race'; and after his first two races, he always started long odds-on and faced an average of three rivals. Provideo had to do things the hard way most times.

For instance, Provideo ran on 16 different courses, often journeying to the north of England; he had few easy races, and, unlike The Bard, was occasionally asked to tackle some of the best of his age. In terms of merit his peak performances came when he won the Star Stakes at Sandown by four lengths, and finished a close second in the Lanson Champagne Stakes at Goodwood and the Prince of Wales's Stakes at York.

If Provideo was not out of the top drawer, no one could deny his courage and tenacity, for he usually made all the running, and having picked up extra weight for his wins, he was usually taken on by at least one horse who was carrying less. That was particularly the case in a valuable race at Haydock in July, when Provideo looked like being swamped by two more-than-capable rivals but he battled on to win by a short head and a neck.

Provideo averaged one win every ten days up to midsummer, and beat the twentieth-century record of 13 jointly held by Nagwa (1975) and Spindrifter (1980) in that grand-sounding race at Ripon on 27 August. Though there was plenty of time to the end of the season, the options were running out. British race conditions are not framed to allow one horse to dominate race after race, hence the skill O'Gorman displayed in finding the right targets and getting Provideo to them.

A five-horse race at Doncaster on 26 October brought up win No. 15, and so to Redcar. It was make or break for Provideo, since he had no other engagement in this country before the season ended on 10 November. Five took him on but by halfway he was clear of them, and driven out to the line by Ives he won by seven lengths.

Provideo went to California later in the month and was given one chance to beat The Bard. He failed, but if he had decided enough was enough, who could blame him? (His feat was matched by Timeless Times in 1990.)

Ever Ready Derby Stakes, 1985

Won by Slip Anchor – Epsom, Wednesday 5 June

Making the running as a means of winning the Derby went out of fashion when Steve Donoghue hung up his boots in 1937. The American jockey Bill Shoemaker surprised everybody on Hawaiian Sound in 1978 and was caught only in the dying stages, but he had an excuse for the tactics; it was his first ride in England! Then along came Slip Anchor and Steve Cauthen, another rider who gained his grounding in the States. They tore up the textbook and won by seven lengths.

Slip Anchor had won his two races prior to Epsom but had not beaten a top-class horse in either. He had, however, shown he enjoyed racing from the front, at which Cauthen is expert, and that he was improving fast. His trainer Henry Cecil had not entertained serious thoughts about his being a Derby horse until he ran away with the Lingfield Trial on his third outing of the season.

He started favourite at Epsom in a smaller-than-usual field of 14. The rest might well have stayed at home for all the chance they had once Slip Anchor came out of the stalls in front. Engaging easily into gear, Slip Anchor was soon in command and Cauthen made no attempt to restrain him. There was no need to put on the brakes; Slip Anchor had proved he stayed a mile and a half and since he did not have the ability to

The one-horse Derby, in which Slip Anchor makes every yard of the running and comes home seven lengths clear of Law Society. The rest, led by Damister and Supreme Leader, were in another parish.

quicken that others possessed, the best ploy was to use his strong galloping quality to the full.

As the course began to wind down and round Tattenham Hill, Cauthen asked Slip Anchor to quicken the pace, and turning into the straight he was ten lengths clear of Petoski, who shaded Phardante and Supreme Leader, with the second favourite Law Society pocketed in fifth place. The race was already won, though there were still three and a half furlongs to travel.

Slip Anchor kept up his relentless gallop and, with Cauthen taking no chances, he beat the late-finishing Law Society by the same margin that Troy had defeated Dickens Hill by six years earlier. Only the ten-length winner Shergar and Manna, who won by eight lengths for Donoghue in 1925, had won by farther, but no other Derby winner has put 13 lengths between himself and the third-placed finisher, as Slip Anchor did.

The time for the race was good but the style of winning was better, and it brought a first Derby success for trainer Cecil, jockey Cauthen and owner-breeder Lord Howard de Walden, who had been seeking to produce a winner of the race for 38 years. By coincidence Lord Howard came up with one in the year that his tip-top miler Kris was champion sire. Slip Anchor was by the 1978 Derby winner Shirley Heights, who in turn was by Mill Reef, the winner in 1971. 'Watch out for a son of Slip Anchor in 1995' is an obvious message.

Any attempts to turn Slip Anchor into a world-beater on the strength of his Epsom effort soon proved groundless. He never won again, largely because of a combination of being taken on by horses with superior speed and appearing to grow tired of attempts to make him settle behind a pacemaker. But he remains one of the best Derby winners of the period, and having been given a rating of 135 by the official handicappers in their International Classifications, he has only eight ahead of him in an order of merit which first appeared in 1977. Three of those are Derby winners – Shergar (140), Generous (137) and Troy (136).

An owner-breeder's fondest hopes are fulfilled as Lord Howard de Walden leads in his Derby winner Slip Anchor.

Tote Cheltenham Gold Cup, 1986

Won by Dawn Run – Thursday 13 March

Agony and ecstasy: it's a cliche which headline writers attempt to avoid but seldom can. It fits perfectly the story of Dawn Run in 1986. In March she returned to the thundering cheers of a massive crowd after winning the Cheltenham Gold Cup; in June she lay dead on France's premier jumping course.

Dawn Run is the only horse to have won both the Champion Hurdle and the Cheltenham Gold Cup, and no one who was there, or watching on television, the day she completed the double will forget the thrill, the excitement and the scenes of joy.

For three days in March Cheltenham becomes home for the Irish. They have had

Dawn Run is a length down on Forgive 'N Forget (left) and Wayward Lad at the last fence but she fights back for a famous victory.

some great times at the Festival meeting; more recently they have had some lean ones. But when Dawn Run and Jonjo O'Neill, Irish to the core, won the Gold Cup, they had a glorious day. British racing fans joined in the celebrations, for Dawn Run had captured everyone's imagination.

Ridden by O'Neill, she won the Champion Hurdle in 1984, starting odds-on in a field of 14 and beating the long-shot Cima by three-quarters of a length. It was not her best form but she had become the first mare to win the race since 1939. O'Neill did not ride her again in public until the 1986 Gold Cup. Plenty happened in the meantime.

There's little to be seen of Dawn Run and Jonjo O'Neill as the Cheltenham crowd show their feelings.

The partnership was broken only because O'Neill was injured, and trainer Paddy Mullins' son Tony returned. Mullins junior had ridden Dawn Run in most of her early races, though her redoubtable owner Charmian Hill was in the saddle for her first three outings. Mrs Hill might have gone on longer, but the Irish Turf authorities politely refused to grant her a licence. She was 62!

Back together, Tony Mullins and Dawn Run won five races on the trot, including the most important hurdle race in France, the Grande Course de Haies at Auteuil, and her first three steeplechases. Dawn Run had a year's gap between two of the races because of a leg injury, but she came back as sound as a bell and she and Mullins seemed to be proceeding steadily to the top of a new tree.

That was before she went to Cheltenham in January 1986 to get her eye in for the Gold Cup, which she would be tackling after very little chasing experience. At the sixteenth fence, six from the finish, where she was well clear, she stood off too far, clouted the fence and shot Mullins to the ground. He caught her and remounted for a distant fourth place, but the damage was done. Mrs Hill wanted a change of rider, and O'Neill climbed back.

Despite being the least experienced runner, but prompted by the absence of Burrough Hill Lad, Dawn Run started favourite against ten rivals for the Gold Cup. For 13 fences she jumped like an old hand, measuring strides with the habitual front-runner Run And Skip, but then she lost ground with a mistake at the water jump. She was soon back on terms, but again lost her place with an error at the eighteenth fence, five from the finish.

The Dawn Run statue stands proudly overlooking the scene of her Cheltenham triumphs.

Running down the hill into the final straight, Dawn Run was on the inside, picking up ground on the strong-running leaders Wayward Lad and Forgive 'N Forget, and a good jump at the second-last took her to the front. She did not quicken away from the fence as well as the other two and at the last obstacle was a length down. She was two lengths adrift halfway up the run-in but did not give up, and with O'Neill driving, and the whole of Ireland seemingly cheering, she forged a length ahead of Wayward Lad for a famous victory.

Cheltenham had not witnessed scenes like those which greeted Dawn Run. The winner's enclosure teemed with people desperate to salute their hero. Mrs Hill was hoisted shoulder high; so too was O'Neill, who later raised Tony Mullins on to his own shoulders to join the fun.

Three months and four races later, on a hot day in Paris, Dawn Run was dead, killed by a broken neck in a fall at the fifth-last flight in the Grande Course de Haies. Some of the heart went out of National Hunt racing that day.

Breeders' Cup Classic, 1987

Won by Ferdinand – Hollywood Park, California, Saturday 21 November

At the end of a race which made the heart beat faster Ferdinand (rails) holds on to beat Alysheba by a nose.

As the setting for seven world championship events in one afternoon, the Breeders' Cup series still has considerable progress to make towards that billing. As an unrivalled spectacle of top-class racing and razzmatazz, it is there already.

Conceived by the leading US owner and breeder John R Gaines, the Breeders' Cup programme was aimed at promoting American horseracing within the States but beyond its narrow publicity confines. The vehicle was a set of races which added up to the richest fixture in the world, with the intention of bringing together the best in America, as well as top horses from around the world, in a mix of races – dirt and turf, two-year-old and older, filly and colt, sprint and mile and middle-distance.

Major funding came from breeders, and they produced a total prize fund of $10 million, a staggering advance on anything previously offered for one day's racing anywhere in the world.

The inaugural championship event was run at Hollywood Park, California, in

It was billed as a showdown between the generations and that's how it turned out once Alysheba (left) had forged through to join battle with Ferdinand.

November 1984. The crowd of 64,254 bet almost $8.5 million on the seven races, and a further $8 million was wagered off course around the country. There were 68 runners, including nine from Europe – three from France, four from Britain and two from Ireland – and Lashkari won the Breeders' Cup Turf over a mile and a half for the Aga Khan and Alain de Royer-Dupre. In the second year, at Aqueduct in New York, Clive Brittain's filly Pebbles won the Turf; and in the third, at Santa Anita in California, the French-trained colt Last Tycoon took the Mile.

It was a satisfactory start for European interests, and though there were huge drawbacks – climate, distance, unfamiliar tracks and racing conditions, and time of year, for example – the attraction grew. When the event returned to Hollywood Park in 1987, there were 14 runners from Europe; nine from Britain and five from France.

The strongest challenge was in the Mile, and Europe supplied the first two favourites in Sonic Lady, who had had a light season, and Miesque, who had been campaigned since the spring. Miesque and Freddy Head were brilliant, hugging the rails as if they had raced in the States all their lives and coming home three and a half lengths clear.

Miesque's was a magnificent performance, almost capped an hour later by the Arc winner Trempolino, who was beaten only half a length by the ex-Irish-trained five-year-old Theatrical in the Turf. Two marvellous races, but there was better to come, and there wasn't a European horse within 30 lengths of the main action.

The Classic had all the ingredients to be a great race: top prize-money of the day, totalling $3 million; and the last two Kentucky Derby winners, Ferdinand and Alysheba, trained by two legends of US racing, Charlie Whittingham and Jack Van Berg, and ridden by two of the country's finest jockeys, Bill Shoemaker and Chris McCarron.

It lived up to its promise, and more, as Ferdinand and Alysheba raced hammer and tongs down the straight, nose to nose in the last half-furlong. Shoemaker came three horses wide round the last turn, setting Ferdinand hard on the quarters of the two leaders, while McCarron brought Alysheba from farther back and wider to challenge. Shoemaker was determined not to hit the front too soon, for fear that Ferdinand would relax, and it was only 150 yards from the finish that he asked him to quicken into the lead. All the time, Alysheba was closing, and they virtually raced as one for the last 50 yards. The verdict was a nose in favour of Ferdinand.

'He got the job done,' said Shoemaker. 'It was a very tough one to lose,' sighed McCarron. It was a great race to watch.

Ladbrokes (Ayr) Gold Cup Handicap, 1988

Won by So Careful – Friday 16 September

Most Flat-race trainers would nominate the Derby, or a race at Royal Ascot, or one of the top middle-distance events, as the race they most want to win. Jack Berry dreamed of winning the Ayr Gold Cup.

He had harboured the ambition ever since he was a teenager in the early 1950s, apprenticed to trainer Charlie Hall at Towton in his native Yorkshire. Hall trained some of the best jumpers in the North, but the young Berry came into contact with Flat horses because Towser Gosden, sending runners from his stables at Lewes in Sussex to Ayr, would lodge them briefly with Hall. When the Gosden string needed loosening-up exercise alongside Hall's more stoutly bred jumpers, the lightweight Berry would volunteer.

Berry thrilled to the speed of the Flat-

Everything after this is a bonus for trainer Jack Berry as So Careful wins from Chaplins Club, Foolish Touch and Restore.

racers, and it has fascinated him ever since. More recently he has made it his trademark, though when he gave up being a hard-working but only moderately successful jump jockey to start training in 1969, speed was usually the last quality his small stable of horses revealed. They were mainly hurdlers and chasers, and modest ones at that. But he did well with the material at his disposal, and his horses always turned up at the races looking immaculate.

It was when he moved across the Pennines in 1974 to start training at Cockerham, near Lancaster, that he began to build up the speed theme. National Hunt horses were still his mainstay but the inevitable breakdowns hurt him. He knew all about the frailty of jumpers from his riding days, but while a jockey can walk away from a lame horse, a trainer has him on the premises as a constant reminder.

Berry decided to change tack, and his first Flat winner – Fiona's Pet, ridden by his wife Jo in an amateur riders' sprint race – set the pace. She had speed, and that was what Berry was looking for. He has found it in increasing numbers, gradually at first but more spectacularly in the last four years, in sharp, sprint-bred horses bought mainly at the Doncaster Sales, where he could purchase yearlings with good conformation and an attractive price tag.

Ironically, the horse who realized Berry's greatest ambition went to Cockerham as a four-year-old at the request of his Irish owner-breeder. So Careful had failed to win in Ireland but Berry managed to pick up one race with him in his first season and two more – including a farcical match against an elderly horse whose owner thought, erroneously, that he could beat the world speed record – before he went to Ayr for the Gold Cup.

Berry had had runners in the race before, and they had made a bold show, but not bold enough. So Careful was the exception. Ridden by Nicky Carlisle and starting at 33–1 in a maximum field of 29, he was always handily placed, was sent to the front almost two furlongs from the finish and tidily held the late run of Chaplins Club by a length.

Jack Berry has made a big name for himself with two-year-olds and sprinters.

'After that, everything else is a bonus,' Berry told those who asked him to identify his next target. And there have been plenty of bonuses, for Berry has spotted a gap and gone for it. He has plotted the season's two-year-old races, and made it his business to have the horses ready to run in as many as possible.

So Careful contributed to Berry's score of 70 winners on the Flat in 1988. Since then the annual totals have been 92, 127 and 143, and in each of the last two seasons he has had more winners than any other trainer. In 1990, 87 of his wins were in two-year-old races; in 1991 the figure was increased to 90. His aim is to have 100 two-year-old winners. But it's not such a burning ambition as was winning the Ayr Gold Cup.

William Hill Claiming Stakes (Div 1), 1989

Won by Niklas Angel – Lingfield Park, Monday 30 October

They're off, and about to make a piece of racing history in the first all-weather track race run in Britain.

Britain gave organized horse racing to the world, showed it how to run the business, and then sat back. The rest of the world got on with the job of making progress, and Britain has picked up ideas from all over the place. Photo-finish, starting stalls and overnight declaration of runners are just three areas in which Britain followed the field. All-weather track racing is the latest.

American horses race predominantly on a man-made surface, since the structure of the Stateside programme, with courses staging day after day of racing for months on end, makes anything more than a limited amount of turf racing impossible. In the colder parts of Europe there is no chance of racing in winter without finding an alternative to turf.

For long enough Britain put up with inclement weather and the inevitable abandonment of racing as if it were an unavoidable part of the cycle. It was, as long as there was no alternative.

A run of bad winters, culminating in the loss of 72 days' racing in the first two months of 1985, prompted a bright spark in the Jockey Club to suggest it might be worth looking for an alternative. When there was no racing, there was no betting; and when there was no betting, there was no money coming in from the bookmakers through the Levy. More than that, if the blank days went on long enough, punters might start looking elsewhere for their pleasure, to greyhounds for instance. They might take some persuading to come back to horseracing.

The Jockey Club set up a working party chaired by 'Monkey' Blacker, the deputy senior steward, and in November 1985 it gave the all-clear for the idea of building at least one all-weather track. It would provide guaranteed racing for a period through the worst of the winter, and would help to offset the loss of betting revenue caused by abandonments.

It was in the Levy Board's interest to support the scheme and it came up with considerable financial assistance. Finding a racecourse to take up the offer was a bigger problem. Kempton showed interest but pulled out on the grounds that it would have to tear up one of its turf courses, and Doncaster thought better of the idea when its pleas for extra cash fell on deaf ears. Nottingham was thrust into and out of the limelight when Ron Muddle made an unsuccessful bid for the track on behalf of his company, RAM Racecourses. Eventually, and rather late in the day, the choice fell on Lingfield, which was always in the running but had been sold by Mr Muddle to another company, and Southwell, which Mr Muddle had bought after a Christmas Eve bid to the shareholders.

In April 1989 construction of the Equitrack surface at Lingfield began, and approval was given for the use of a Fibresand surface at Southwell. The two courses had six months to get ready for their first all-weather meetings – Lingfield on the Flat on 30 October, and Southwell over hurdles two days later.

After a cautious and sometimes criticized start, all-weather track racing is already part of the scenery.

Neither course had an easy ride on the way to bringing in all-weather. Time was short; building had to be done; trials had to be carried out on the surfaces, and no one knew how much support they would get from owners and trainers. It might have been commonplace overseas, but this was fresh territory for conservative Britain.

As far as the first day was concerned, too many wanted to get involved. Races had to be divided and a six-race card doubled in size overnight. Racing went on from 11 in the morning till 4.30 in the afternoon, and the first name on the scoresheet was Niklas Angel, a three-year-old trained at Newmarket by Conrad Allen and ridden by Richard Quinn, who made sure he too went in the record books by riding the second winner, Consulate, for Peter Makin.

After three seasons, all-weather Flat racing is so well established that Britain no longer has a natural break, but all-weather hurdle racing is finding it hard to take root, simply because – by Murphy's Law – all-weather has been followed by open weather in winter and there has been no requirement to switch turf-proven hurdlers to dirt. Refinements will be made but all-weather, in one form or other, is here to stay.

Tote Cheltenham Gold Cup, 1990

Won by Norton's Coin – Thursday 15 March

Toby Tobias (left) is foot perfect; Desert Orchid makes a mistake, but Norton's Coin is waiting to pounce.

Sirrell Griffiths milked his herd of Friesian cows a little earlier than usual on Thursday one week, and a little later than usual on Friday. In between he won the Cheltenham Gold Cup.

It was meant to be another celebration of Desert Orchid's majesty; instead it turned into another fairy-tale in the history of National Hunt racing and the biggest upset in the history of the Gold Cup. Sirrell Griffiths trained three horses under permit on his farm at Nantgaredig near Carmarthen, and one of them, Norton's Coin, won the 1990 Gold Cup at 100–1.

Perhaps the state of the going had something to do with the result, for the starting price of Norton's Coin was not the only record. His winning time was the fastest ever registered for the distance, beating by 4.4 seconds the record set by Dawn Run in the same race in 1986. Ten of the 18 winners during the three-day meeting beat the clock, illustrating that the going was unusually fast for this time of year.

They went a good clip from the start of the Gold Cup, as the odds-on Desert Orchid took them along in his usual enthusiastic style. But he was never able to get far in front because Ten of Spades kept him in his sights from the start and had the audacity to take the lead with six fences to jump. Desert Orchid reasserted himself three fences later, but having been forced slightly wide round the final turn, he gave way to Toby Tobias.

But who was the chestnut horse jumping the last within half a length of the leader, and a length ahead of the tired Desert Orchid? It was none other than the Welsh wonder, Norton's Coin, who had always been handily placed for Graham McCourt and now looked assured of at least second prize. That would have been one place higher than Griffiths hoped for when he set out for Cheltenham that morning, but there was better to come.

Straining every muscle as they raced up the hill, both horses gave everything. McCourt gave a little more and, with his jockey's whip beating out encouragement, Norton's Coin put in a strong run which carried him to the front in the last 100 yards. He won by three-quarters of a length from Toby Tobias, with Desert Orchid, a bit-player in the final drama, four lengths away in third place.

McCourt had some of the shine wiped off his victory with a visit to the stewards' room. The officials were not best pleased by his use of the whip and suspended him for three days for using the aid, in their words, 'with a degree of severity which injured his horse'. Whip abuse has become a much discussed issue of the moment, with the Jockey Club seeking to counter public criticism and protect the sport's image. Some jump jockeys have yet to take the hint.

The irony is that Norton's Coin himself considerably enhanced the image of National Hunt racing. At a time when money has come to mean more and more in racing, and professionalism is the key word, his arrival in the headlines was a breath of fresh air.

Initially his ruddy-faced owner, from the grass roots of the sport, seemed bemused by all the attention but he quickly took it in his stride. He was neither embarrassed nor annoyed that no one seemed to know him, and was willing to supply the missing details in a charming and unassuming manner. His finest hour might not have been a good result for punters, but it did jump racing no harm at all.

Surprise turns to smiles as Graham McCourt gives his version of events to Sirrell Griffiths, trainer of Norton's Coin, and his wife.

Breeders' Cup Juvenile, 1991

Won by Arazi – Churchill Downs, Kentucky, Saturday 2 November

It was the most astonishing, awe-inspiring race this writer has ever seen. So astonishing that it is worth recording what unbiased American observers thought of Arazi when he won the richest two-year-old race in the northern hemisphere.

Journalist Ed Fountaine, in the *Daily Racing Form*: 'A performance that was so dominating and electrifying that he was immediately compared to Secretariat.'

Bruce Headley, trainer of the runner-up Bertrando: 'He is a monster. He reminds me of Secretariat or Swaps.'

Trainer Shug McGaughey: 'Arazi's performance was one of the greatest I've ever seen by a two-year-old.'

Jockey Mike Smith, who rode fourth-placed Offbeat: 'Early on he acted like he didn't know what to do. Then he got down to business and annihilated them.'

Jockey Alex Solis, who rode Bertrando: 'At the half-mile pole I was sitting there with a lot of horse and just wasn't prepared for somebody to run by me. That's just an incredible horse.'

Journalist Tony Cobitz, in the *Racing Times*: 'The truly spectacular manner of his victory really had nothing to do with time. This was the rarest kind of top-class display.'

Trainer D Wayne Lukas: 'Toss him all his bouquets, give him his time in the sun. When you look at everything he had to

Arazi annihilates the field, and America had seen nothing like it since Secretariat.

overcome, you've got to give him a lot of credit.'

Lukas got to the point in one. Winning by five lengths was one thing; doing it on foreign soil and on an unfamiliar dirt surface, after flying in from France, was another; but it was the way Arazi won which drew the gasps.

Drawn on the wide outside of 14, Arazi was steadied by Pat Valenzuela to negotiate the first turn safely as Bertrando made the running. Switching to the inside, Valenzuela took Arazi to the rails but halfway down the back straight he was all of 15 lengths behind the leader. As he began to pick up horses Valenzuela wove his way between them, and Arazi responded with amazing nimbleness, all the while surging forward with no apparent effort.

He made up ground so quickly around the final bend that within a matter of strides he was on the heels of Bertrando, and in a few more seconds he was sweeping past him on the outside. Arazi flew by; yet still he had not finished, for as he homed in on the rails he surged ten lengths ahead. In the last half-furlong Valenzuela eased down, otherwise his winning margin might have been doubled.

The reaction from the packed crowd was instant. As Arazi raced into the final furlong there was a spontaneous burst of applause and appreciation which the locals say is usually reserved only for the Kentucky Derby. That's what the Americans, and the host of European visitors, thought about it.

Considering that trainer François Boutin, the most enthusiastic European supporter of the Breeders' Cup, had not been overkeen to send Arazi to Churchill Downs, his performance was all the more remarkable. It was only on the insistence of owner Allen Paulson, who also won the Mile with Opening Verse, that Arazi made the trip.

Arazi had already guaranteed his place as the best European two-year-old by winning his last six races in France, including the elusive four-timer of Prix Robert Papin, Prix Morny, Prix de la Salamandre and Grand Criterium. His American adventure, which counted in the International Classification reckoning, thrust him even higher in that order of merit. His rating of 130 is the best ever recorded for a two-year-old. In January he was awarded top weight of 130lb in the American equivalent, the Experimental Free Handicap, becoming the first horse to top the list on both sides of the Atlantic. Not since Bold Lad in 1964 has such a high weight been handed out, even to Secretariat. The figures confirmed what those who were privileged to be at Churchill Downs thought.

A job well done for Pat Valenzuela, who salutes Arazi's victory (above), and trainer François Boutin, who takes the reins as the colt's lad washes down the wonder horse (left).

INDEX

This index lists horses, jockeys, owners and trainers. The names of horses are shown in **bold**.